GROWING UP
CHICANA/O

Other **GROWING UP** *Titles*

GROWING UP CHICANA/O

EDITED AND WITH AN INTRODUCTION BY

TIFFANY ANA LÓPEZ

FOREWORD BY RUDOLFO ANAYA

Perennial

An Imprint of HarperCollinsPublishers

Permissions, constituting a continuation of the copyright page, appear on pages 270 to 272.

A hardcover edition of this book was published in 1993 by William Morrow.

HarperCollins books may be purchased for educational, business, or sales promotional use. For information please write: Special Markets Department, HarperCollins Publishers Inc., 10 East 53rd Street, New York, NY 10022.

First Avon edition published 1995.

Reprinted in Perennial 2003.

The Library of Congress has catalogued the hardcover edition as follows:
  Growing up Chicana/o: an anthology / edited and with an introduction by Tiffany Ana López: foreword by Rudolfo Anaya.
    p. cm.
1. American literature—Mexican American authors. 2. Mexican American women—Literary collections. 3. Girls—United States—Literary collections. 4. American literature—Women authors. 5. American literature—20th century. I. López, Tiffany Ana. II. Title: Growing up Chicano.
PS508.M4G76   1993   93-28195
810.8'092—dc20   CIP
[B]

ISBN 0-380-72419-7 (pbk.)

03 04 05 06 07 RRD 10 9 8

FOREWORD

GROWING UP IS ONE OF THE UNIVERSAL THEMES IN LITERATURE. IT is during the childhood years that our values are formed by family and community. It is also a time when we acquire many of the basic skills we will use later in life. For the child or the teenager, growing up is a series of new experiences, emotions, relationships, and the awareness of sexuality. Everything about growing up is more intense and heartfelt.

Writers often need to describe the world of their childhood. We believe that by writing about growing up we can give meaning to those tumultuous years. That is how I felt when I wrote my first novel, *Bless Me, Ultima*. It was important to capture in a story the swirl of emotions and experiences that shaped my growing-up years.

Our growing-up stories provide a history of our past, and in so doing they illuminate the present. *The Adventures of Huckleberry Finn* and *Tom Sawyer* are classics not only because of the wonderful characters but because they provide a history of the times and thus inform us of the world of the author.

It is important for each generation to read the growing-up stories of previous generations, and thus acquire the touchstone by which to chart a course for the future. Each one of us remembers the stories, written or in the oral tradition, that affected us as children. Those stories fired our imagination, filled us with wonder, and allowed us to understand our place in the world. Those stories also taught us that each one of us is a storyteller, each one of us is a creative human being.

The act of storytelling is very important in the Chicano community. Listening to or reading stories leads one to become a storyteller, and in writing a story one can re-create one's life. For the more than eighteen million Mexican Americans living in the United States, the growing-up years have been a mixture of joy, frustration, pain, and a search for identity. Our history, language, literature, and the Chicano Movement of the 1960s are important elements that make us a distinct community.

It was during the Chicano Movement of the 1960s that many Mexican Americans decided to call themselves Chicanos. By naming themselves they took on a new awareness of their place in society. Chicanos began to take pride in their mestizo heritage, pride in both their European and Indian history. It became important during those years to preserve the Spanish language and many of the traditions that were being lost as the force of assimilation led more and more into the mainstream culture.

During the sixties and seventies the Chicano community struggled for more civil rights and equality. We looked back on our history and reminded the world that our European ancestors had been in the southwest United States since 1540 when Coronado marched into what is now New Mexico. During those important explorations the language of commerce and education in the region became Spanish. Spanish has been spoken in the area of the present-day United States since long before Jamestown, the first permanent English settlement, was founded in 1607.

From Texas to California, the rich mother heritage that is Mexican in origin has spawned the culture we call Chicano today. It is a Hispanic culture because of the language, and even though there are many regional differences, elements like history, language, religion, food, fiestas, and other ceremonies keep the core of the culture intact. Whether our ancestors were the first Españoles or Mexicanos who settled the Southwest or the newly arrived immigrant from Mexico, we all are heirs to the same common history.

Unfortunately, the history we read in school has often not included or portrayed the Chicano community of the Southwest, and it has certainly not portrayed those who have sought work in the migrant streams that took them up into the Midwest and the Northwest where they, too, have founded branches of the Chicano community. The family of the Mexican Americans has grown, it has spread to many places, and yet everywhere the common elements still exist.

What is history? And why have we been left out of the history books? For me, history includes the daily life of people, and it is written in their stories, poems, songs, and corridos, and in their daily communication. Historians have often not looked at these sources, or their narrow prejudices have kept them from taking note of the important contributions Mexican Americans have made to this land.

Chicano writers and historians are setting the record straight. In these stories, which Tiffany Ana López has collected, you will find a special slice of Chicano history. It is a creative history, told in the form of stories, and it deals with that special time of youth. Enjoy the stories for what they are, creative works, but keep in mind they also allow you a view into the Chicano world.

We know from the stories we read in school, from newspapers, magazines, television, radio, and even from the advertising media, what it means to grow up in white America. For many Chicanos in this country, those experiences of growing up were a fantasy. They did not speak directly to our experience.

It is fair to say that as long as our literature was not available to white America, this country did not really know the life of the Chicano community. A book like this helps open a window to a part of the life of Chicanos. You may be surprised to learn

that the same issues that concern the Chicano writers concern
all readers. The stories are about growing up, encountering
love, school life, life in the barrio, making friends.

You will also find more attention given to the family; la
familia and all the relationships involved therein are very important in Chicano literature. The relationship with the elders
in a family provides a valuable learning context for our younger
generation. The elders are the roots of our cultural ways. You
will find important attention given to the theme of identity. We
know who we are and we know our history, but belonging to
an ethnic group within the confines of the wider society makes
it necessary for us constantly to affirm this identity. This push
and pull between the world of our own culture and the larger
Anglo American world provides our literature with important
subject matter.

How we relate to each other in this multicultural society is a
theme in the stories. Having lived the role of a minority ethnic
group within the society, Chicano writers have important things
to say about the experience. So you may find more attention
given to racial or ethnic prejudices and bigotry and how it affects
people.

The voice of the woman writer in these stories should draw
special attention. Chicano culture is patriarchal in orientation,
and as more and more Chicanas write they influence not only
the content of the literature but also the culture itself. If literature
is a liberating experience, then the voice of the Chicana writer
in our culture is one of the most influential in helping to shape
and change the cultural ways.

Language, like history, is at the heart of these stories. For
Chicanos, one community within the larger Spanish-speaking
world of the Americas, Spanish is the mother tongue. Our
ancestors spoke Spanish, and so the language became the unify-
ing element of our culture. Today, many of the young people
are not keeping up the practice of speaking Spanish, and yet
they are still historically connected to the language.

A contemporary question for Chicano writers has been whether to write in Spanish or English. We know that in order to be published in this country, Chicano writers have to write in English. There is a big audience of Spanish readers in this country, but very little effort by publishers to publish for those readers. There are also other forces at work that have dictated that Chicano writers write in English.

More and more the language used at home is English. Survival at school and in the workplace dictate that one must speak English. Many of the stories told by Chicano writers take place in a Spanish-speaking setting, for example, at home or in the barrio, but the story is told in English. This has created unique problems for Chicano writers.

Some writers use a technique called code-switching, a bilingual approach to the story. The story is largely written in English, but at appropriate times Spanish is used. This technique reminds the reader the world of the Chicano is bilingual, shifting back and forth between Spanish and English. I have heard some readers complain that the bilingual use of language in stories interferes with the reading of the story; I suggest this technique is a creative use of language that enhances the stories.

The setting and ambience of the stories also remind the reader they are in a barrio or in a Chicano home. At times the stories enter into a realm that critics have labeled magical realism. The entering of this magical plane has been common in the style and content of Latin American literature, and it is common to Chicano writers.

Storytelling is communication. In this collection you will have an opportunity to observe how Chicanos feel about their world; you will also see how they relate to the Anglo American world. If Chicanos and Anglo Americans are to understand each other better, then these stories are one way toward that eventual understanding.

Cultural groups that live next to each other affect each other. Since the war between the United States and Mexico ended in

1848, the Spanish-speaking Mexican community and the Anglo Americans have occupied the same land. This theme is woven into the stories. Perhaps learning how we "can all get along" is one of the most important functions of literature.

Contemporary Chicano literature has come a long way since the first poets and writers joined César Chávez in the fields of California to protest the unequal treatment Chicano and other workers received. In the short span of a quarter century Chicano literature has blossomed. Written in English, it now assumes a place in the literature of the United States. With its historical relationship to Mexico and its grounding in the Southwest, it also still speaks to the Latino world south of Mexico. It is in many ways the bridge across la frontera, joining Anglo America to Latin America.

The writers in this collection represent that bridge. You will continue to hear from these writers, for they are professionals dedicated to their art. Their voices and their works will continue to grow in clarity and expression. Their reputations will grow, as will the body of Chicano literature.

—*Rudolfo Anaya*

ACKNOWLEDGMENTS

LIKE CHICANA/O CULTURE, THIS ANTHOLOGY IS WOVEN FROM many sources of support. There are so many people to acknowledge for their direct and indirect support of this project that I cannot thank enough all who provided thoughts, work, encouragement, and advice. I would like to publicly thank the following people for their labor y corazón:

My research assistant and friend Toni Brent for all of her contributions and insights that did what I could not have done alone; my AMAC group, who helped me hear the voices; Kathleen Baggarley por mi alma y salud; Raquel Quiroz González at the Colección Tloque Nahuaque, University of California at Santa Barbara (UCSB), for her patience and permissions. Francisco Lomelí for his recommendations and council; Rudolfo Anaya for his continual support and involvement in this project and others; my editor Will Schwalbe for all of his advice, encouragement, and support; and B.A. for the promise of the vision.

I would also like to thank the following people for having read and commented on drafts: Darryl Carr, Emily Allen, and, most especially, Elena Craviotto. Muchisimo gracias por Duarte Silva of Stanford University and the audience of teachers at the California Foreign Language Project who provided feedback and support for this anthology. You helped me shape and direct this for you and your classes.

To Olivia Castellano, mi madre, friend, and guide. Antonia Casteñeda for "corazón de melon," the Chicana/o Graduate Students at UCSB in that historical seminar of spring 1993; mil gracias to mi compañeras Melinda Ramirez and Magdalena Torres for la información! Matt Garland and mi colega Alma Rosa Alvarez for their ears as I talked through the various stages of the drafts; Mario García and Ellen McCracken for their support and information; Tere Romo for "Cosas From Louie The Foot González"; Susan Bergholz for her work and support of this project and the promotion of the literature; Cindy Speigel, Carl Gutiérrez-Jones, Shirley Geok-lin Lim, Paddy Fumerton, Alan Liu, and Giles Gunn for all their practical advice on the theory-versus-praxis end of things.

For the final mix, thank you and great appreciation for: Zachary Schisgal at Morrow por todo, Jennifer Cheung Photography of Los Angeles, the children at St. Andrew's Grammar School in Pasadena, Yolanda Broyles-Gonzalez for her summer tortilla talks, and P.L. for all his help and support, con mucho cariño.

I most especially want to thank all the writers in this anthology—particularly for the time and attention given to discuss their works and childhood, which added the salsa to this collection. I would also like to thank all the presses involved in their permissions for their support and advancement of Chicana/o literature. And to those who have contributed to the ongoing project of collaboration, comunidad y mas.

CONTENTS

INTRODUCTION

LIKE EVERY YOUNG CHILD, I WAS READ FAIRY TALES ABOUT CINDER-
ella, Snow White, and Little Red Riding Hood. But I also was
told stories about growing up that had nothing to do with the
experiences of the characters in those fairy tales. *Mi abuelita* and
mis tías would tell me the tales of La Llorona, the weeping
woman who wandered the river banks, howling for the children
she had thrown into the waters. However, as much as I read, I
never found their stories within the pages of a book you could
order through school or on the shelves of the neighborhood
library.

When I was growing up Chicana, I never read anything in
school by anyone who had a *z* in their last name. No González,
no Jiménez, no Chávez, no López. And I grew to accept this
and eventually to stop looking, since no one showed me that
indeed such writers existed. This anthology is, in many ways,
a public gift to that child who was always searching for herself
within the pages of a book. It is a collection of the stories I have
found over the years that address the notion of growing up
Chicana/o. I hope that this anthology will be read by young
people. But this is also for people who want to return to those
childhood spaces that influenced the adults they have become.

When I was growing up, I could find no literature that made me aware of others who shared my cultural experiences. I had to discover these growing-up stories as an adult, with an adult's perspective. Like every child, when I was growing up I felt different. Yet there were definitely things about my life as a Chicana that I didn't dare share. Something as simple as taking a piece of meat wrapped up in a tortilla to school set me apart. I read of children taking their sandwiches to school, yet never in my childhood reading experiences did I read about a child taking a tortilla.

The stories presented here bring me closer to my own sense of self. I grew up with an abuela who had kitchen-table talks with me very much like the one depicted in Rosa Elena Yzquierdo's "Abuela." Mis tías passed on their stories to me in little slips of memory much like the paper moths in Patricia Preciado Martin's "The Ruins." Like any child in any school system, I experienced those moments when teachers are insensitive to the needs and vulnerability of children. I am that child of Sandra Cisneros's "Eleven." I am also that child in Gary Soto's "The Bike," who dared to venture beyond the confines of my neighborhood despite my mother's warnings of danger. I only discovered these shared experiences in a college course in Chicano literature; it was then that my thoughts about growing up Chicana began to come together.

I went to a small state college whose English department was fortunate enough to have a Chicana scholar among its faculty. Having felt that much was missing from her own education and seeing a great need among the Chicana/o students on that campus, Professor Olivia Castellano created a Chicana/o literature course. It was in her class that I read for the very first time many of the writers whose work is presented in this anthology. It was also the first time in my life that I saw my cultural background described in a book assigned for a class. It was electrifying, but at the same time it was terribly sad. It had taken me twenty years to find that part of myself in literature.

To grow up Chicana/o is certainly different than to grow up Cuban, Puerto Rican, Central American, Mexican, or Spanish, to name only a few examples. These cultural groups, often labeled "Latino," do share the Spanish language, but each has its own distinct traditions, foods, dances, art, and literature. In 1965, when the contemporary Chicano Movement began, the sons and daughters of Mexican Americans created the word Chicano to give new meaning to their identity. Chicanos took their destiny in their hands by creating a strong statement of their identity in the arts and by demanding social and political equity within American society. Cultural issues and customs found in the stories in this anthology are what distinguish these works as Chicana/o, along with the fact that the authors included in this anthology are themselves Chicana/o.

In my house, there is a five-foot-long bookshelf that contains all the major works of Chicana/o literature. (Though even as I write this, the shelf continues to expand!) Many of the stories in this anthology are very short. Chicana/o literature has grown out of an oral, as well as poetic, tradition. For many of our ancestors, there was not always the luxury of time needed for a writer's life. The genre of the Chicana/o short story is one in which the writings are concise, well-worked pieces, with much said in a very short space. The writing is also characterized by an autobiographical voice, which continues to be important to members of the community searching for reflections of their own lives within the works.

The collection begins by providing some historical background. The section La Historia: Journeys in the Borderlands includes stories of border culture—Mexico, *el barrio*, boundaries of gender—that provide a framework for many of the stories in the following sections. From the Veins of Los Abuelos includes stories about grandparents. For many of us, our grandparents were our first history teachers, our first storytellers. The mostly school stories in La Tierra y La Escuela: From Where We Learn illustrate those epiphanic moments that produce an immediate feeling of difference and change. The stories in Passages: We Who Are Not As Others focus on the rites of passage that lead to independence and self-awareness. The four sections thus move from stories of community to family to self.

This anthology is not meant to be all-inclusive or totally representative of what it means to be and grow up Chicana/o. These are twenty stories of growth and change that express many different perspectives on a particular cultural experience. I hope that when you leave this book, you will have revisited your own homelands, reexperienced the stories of your own grandparents, reremembered your school days, and the aching desire to be an individual in this society. For many of us, literature was our salvation. It taught us about ourselves and told us what others would not. It was the permission we needed to realize our dreams.

LA HISTORIA:
JOURNEYS
IN THE
BORDERLANDS

Doña Luz continued to explain in a whisper: "This is the history of our people which I have gathered. . . ." She droned on in a cadence, and as she spoke, Alma, still grasping her bony hand and surveying with wonder the testament of Doña Luz, felt the warmth of that hand flow into her being like water being poured. "The recipes, the herbs and the cures; the music and the songs and the dances; the prose and the poems, the sorrows, the joys; the gain and the loss. This is my legacy. But I am old and failing. I entrust it to you lest it be lost and forgotten."

—Patricia Preciado Martin, "The Ruins"

THE RUINS

Patricia Preciado Martin

Patricia Preciado Martin *is the author of* The Legend of the Bellringer of San Agustín, *a bilingual children's story (1980),* Images and Conversations: Mexican Americans Recall a Southwestern Past *(1983; Virginia McCormick Scully Award for best book by a Chicano or Native American writer), and* Songs My Mother Sang to Me: An Oral History of Mexican American Women *(1992). "The Ruins" is from her collection of short stories* Days of Plenty, Days of Want *(1988).*

Oral folklore is an important part of Mexican life; for most Chicanas/os, stories told to us by our familia helped shape us. Legend provides the basis for many stories about the haunting of particular places. Embedded in "The Ruins" are traces of the legend of Atzlán—a promised region where racial injustice, poverty, and old age do not exist.

Martin says of the role history plays in her work: "My memories of growing up Mexicana are very powerful and have been a strong influence as well as a source of inspiration for my writing. We lived in a small mining community south of Tucson for a few years, and the desert and open spaces were my playground. This instilled in me a love of nature and the land. We lived with my grandmother in Barrio Hollywood for a couple of years, and the images there are

still very vivid in my mind—my abuelita's garden, the raspada
vendor, the family gatherings, the devotion of my grandmother to
her santos. The stories of my grandfather's ranch in Mexico became
a minilegend in my family and explain for me my strong ties to the
land. My mother was a great influence in my life—education was
most important to her. We are a very close family—this strong sense
of familia comes from our growing-up years—the required Sunday
visits to my abuelita who didn't speak English. I am proud of my
rich culture; it has made my life varied, interesting, and full."

IT WAS GETTING SO THAT ALMOST EVERY DAY ALMA WAS GOING TO
the ruins on the riverbank. Not that her mother knew, of course.
She was expressly forbidden to go there. It was a place, her
mother Mercedes warned, where winos went on occasion, and
young lovers, frequently. One never knew what kind of mis-
chief or carnal knowledge one might come upon or witness.
When Señora Romero spoke like this—of the proximity of
temptation or occasions of sin—she would finger the large gold
medallion of the Sagrado Corazón that she wore around her
neck and invoke protection for her oldest daughter from the
phalanx of saints with which she was on a first name basis. The
image of the Sagrado Corazón was fortified on the reverse side
with an engraving of the Virgen de Guadalupe, and Señora
Romero wore the medal like the medieval armor of a crusader
prepared to do battle with the infidel. It was a pose Alma saw
her mother strike with frequency—inspired by the worldliness
promoted by newspapers, television, popular music, protes-
tantes, and errant in-laws.

(She was not being disrespectful, Alma had convinced herself,
when her mother would begin her pious sermons, to imagine
Doña Mercedes, a fury on a rearing stallion—lance raised, mail
clanking, banners aloft—routing unbelievers and sinners from
the cantinas and alleyways of South Tucson, until they knelt

trembling and repentant at the vestibule of Santa Cruz Church. Sra. Romero mistook Alma's dreamy unwavering stare for attentiveness, and so these periodic encounters left all parties satisfied. In reality, Sra. Romero never behaved in any manner that would have called attention to herself: decorum, simplicity, and moderation were the measures by which she lived her life and by which she ruled her family.)

It was easy enough for Alma to keep her afternoon sojourns secret from her mother. The excuses were varied and plentiful: extra homework in the library, a dance committee, an after-school game or conference with a teacher. In truth, there was never anything or anyone at school that attracted Alma's attention or detained her there. She was a solitary and thoughtful girl—dutiful in her studies, retiring in her behavior, guarded in her conversation—and so she went unnoticed by her teachers and ignored by the giggling groups of friends that gathered in animated knots in the halls, in the cafeteria, and on the school grounds.

(Alma seemed plain to the casual observer. Her dress was modest, almost dowdy, created from cheap fabric by the nimble fingers of her mother on her Singer treadle sewing machine. She wore no makeup or jewelry, in contrast to her peers at school: with their brightly colored clothes and lips, patterned stockings and flashy plastic accessories, they swarmed through the halls like flocks of rainbow-hued wingless birds. But it could be said that Alma had a certain beauty: she was slim and muscular and lithe, with dark, serious eyes and coppery brown curly hair that obeyed no comb or brush or stylistic whim of her mother. Sra. Romero had long ago given up trying to tame Alma's unruly locks with ribbons and barrettes, abandoning these efforts to dedicate herself to other pursuits that were more pliable to her will.)

Alma always made sure that she arrived home from school at a reasonable hour—in time to help with supper chores or to baby-sit her younger siblings if needed. Sra. Romero never

questioned her tardiness or investigated, satisfied that the delay
of an hour or sometimes two, was taken up with school activi-
ties. A growing family, household duties, and spiritual obligations kept Sra. Romero busy enough. It contented her that
there were no calls from the principal or teachers, and Alma's
excellent grades were testament enough to her industriousness
and trustworthiness. All was well.

Sra. Romero prided herself on the fact that her household
ran so smoothly, and she credited the personal intervention of
the Sagrado Corazón de Jesús for her good fortune. She was
a dedicated and energetic woman who scrubbed, polished,
cooked, washed, ironed, sewed and prayed with great fervor.
Her humble home was spotless, her children orderly, her marriage stable if predictable. Her soul was as spotless as her
house, and it was the former that preoccupied her the most—
but never (and she was scrupulous on this issue) to the neglect
of her domestic duties. Nonetheless, during the week there
always seemed to be a funeral, bautismo or velorio to attend;
a vigil to keep; a manda to complete; a novena or rosary to
recite; a visita to deliver; an altar cloth to iron and mend. And
she was grateful for Alma's good-natured helpfulness around
the house.

In addition to her weekly obligations, on Sunday mornings
Sra. Romero arose faithfully at 5:00 A.M. to go to the Santa Cruz
parish hall to help make menudo with the Guadalupanas to sell
after all the masses. It was recompense enough for her, that,
thanks in part to her pious efforts and sacrifices, the ancient
pastor and his ancient barrio church were solvent. She always
made sure, however, that she was home by nine o'clock to
marshal her immaculate family to church in time to sit in the
front pew at the ten o'clock mass. Her energy in matters spiritual
seemed boundless, and she was admired, and at times envied,
by the other matrons of the southside parish for the sanctity and
punctuality demonstrated by her family.

Alma's father, Sr. José Romero, was a patient and thoughtful man who complied with his wife's spiritual and devotional exigencies without complaining. He had a strong faith, in a manner of speaking, although it had developed more out of philosophical musings and awe of the universe than out of any adherence to theological doctrines. Nonetheless, he faithfully attended church when it was required or politic to do so, and he willingly helped out with repairs at the crumbling church and rectory whenever he could find the time.

Sr. Romero was a good provider whose dependability as a mason for the Estes Homes Construction Company kept his family modestly housed, clothed, and fed. He moonlighted at a Whiting Brothers Gas Station for the extras—music lessons, the yearly trip to California, gifts for special occasions. He himself had few material wants, and, having no interest in money matters, he handed over his paycheck to his thrifty and capable wife who wrought miracles, not only with saints, but with his weekly stipend.

Sr. Romero did, however, always manage to set aside a few dollars for himself from his overtime earnings, which he lavished on his one passion—books. Whenever he could, he would browse among the stacks in the Carnegie Public Library by the park, and he would often check out as many as a dozen books at a time. But Sr. Romero loved most of all wandering among the dusty aisles of the dimly lit used bookstore in the old section of downtown. He would spend hours, when possible, leafing through the musty yellowed volumes, studying the tables of contents and illustrations, fingering the cracked leather bindings embossed with gold lettering. The proprietor, a laconic, prematurely gray-haired man confined to a wheelchair due to a childhood illness, didn't seem to mind. They never spoke, except in greeting, yet in an indefinable way they were the most intimate of companions. Whenever Sr. Romero had accumulated enough savings, he would buy an antique volume or two, and his book collection had grown to the point that it occupied every available shelf and tabletop in their small home. He had taken to caching his books in cardboard boxes under the beds—as long as he kept them neatly stored his orderly wife did not complain.

Sr. Romero read voraciously—in Spanish as well as in English. He seemed to have no literary preferences—poetry, philosophy, history, the natural sciences, fiction, biography—all he consumed with equal fervor. Night after night, he would read in his easy chair after the house had turned quiet—the younger children tucked in bed with prayer, his saintly wife occupied with her evening devotions. Alma would study her father through the doorway while doing her homework at the kitchen table. At times he would pause in his reading and close his book, a finger keeping his place. He would shut his eyes in meditation, his head in a halo of light and smoke, his patrician face composed. Alma alone knew about the tiny flame that burned in the hidden hearth of his soul, and she understood that the flame would flicker with meaningless chatter. He, in turn, sensed in his favorite daughter the very same embers glowing unattended. There was an unspoken pact between them, and thus they kept their silence.

Alma cut west across the football field, as had become her custom. Her backpack dangled loosely on her shoulders—she had left her books behind in her locker, having finished her homework during the lunch hour. Across the field she could see jostling groups of students heading east—crossing the light on South Twelfth Avenue to play video games in the shopping mall or to hang out with Cokes and cigarettes at the Circle K. The less fortunate who had to ride the school buses were crowding and shoving in lines as they embarked. The bus driver, an angular man with a long-suffering face, whose request for a transfer was still sitting on the principal's desk, hunched over the steering wheel in resignation. Alma could see arms flailing out the window in greeting, or directing paper missiles, and she could hear the muffled shouts and catcalls of the students who were good-naturedly elbowing one another for seats.

There was a cut in the chain link fence by the bleachers at the far end of the field. It had been repaired many times, but it never stayed mended, this section of the fence being the most accessible and least detected place for those students wanting free entry to the football games. Alma stepped through the break in the fence and headed north, parallel with the dry riverbed that cut a wide swath between the highway and the school grounds. There was a faint path, but since it was seldom used, except by her, it was overgrown, and the ankle-high weeds and seeds scratched her legs and imbedded themselves in her socks.

She hurried now, because the late November days were getting shorter, and her mother told time by the proximity of the sun to the horizon. It was not cold, but the weakening sun looked hazy and gave an illusion of winter. A gust of wind portending a change in the weather blew unexpectedly out of the south. Alma shivered and wrapped her ill-fitting cardigan more tightly around herself. The path narrowed gradually as she continued north, angling now slightly west toward the slope where she would descend into the riverbed in order to cross to the opposite bank. A few hundred yards farther and she could see across the river to the old mission orchard on the other side—a tangle of denuded trees—peach, apricot, pomegranate, fig and lemon, leafless now and overgrown with wild grape and the vines of the morning glory and the buffalo gourd. On the periphery of the abandoned orchard, the silhouettes of two dead cottonwoods thrust their giant trunks into the sky as if in failed supplication for water. By now Alma could see the decaying walls of the ancient adobe convento, and she could discern the elusive wisp of smoke that arose from somewhere amid the ruins. Far to the southeast, in the direction of the Santa Rita Mountains, she could now see dark clouds dragging their heavy burden over the mountain peaks. If the wind quickened, the storm would be here before dusk.

Alma walked faster now, scrambling down one side of the dry river's eroded bank and up the other, artfully sidestepping the litter of flash flood debris, the broken glass and shiny aluminum of beer busts, discarded construction material and abandoned furniture and car parts. When she had reached the other side of the bank, she brushed her way through a stand of scraggly carrizo and walked over a plank suspended over a narrow ragged cut where the river had meandered decades ago. At last she reached the neglected and overgrown orchard that had become her musing, and lately, her observation place. The trees were gnarled with age and barren now, but even in the spring they boasted few leaves, having to depend on the sparse and unpredictable desert rains for their irrigation. It was nothing short of a wonder that they were still alive: each season seemed to be their last, but now the native shrubs and vines had so intertwined themselves with their sorrowful hosts that they seemed perennially, unnaturally, green.

It was here within view of the ruins that Alma had chosen her secret hiding place: here she would sit day after day on a discarded car seat with broken springs that she had laboriously hauled up from the riverbed. It was from this vantage point that she would observe the comings and goings of the strange old woman who had taken up residence in the crumbling site. They had never spoken, but Alma was sure that the old woman was aware of her presence, and at time she thrilled with the sure knowledge that she, also, was being watched at a distance. It was just a matter of time before their eyes would meet and they would speak. She was sure of it, and her daily watchful ritual was enacted because of the possibility, nay the inevitability, of that encounter.

Doña Luz had squatted at the old ruin since the death of her mother three years before. Although the matriarch of the Martínez family was 97 years old at the time of her death, she had been of robust health and keen of mind and spirit until shortly before her death. When her ancestral family adobe had been bulldozed with the blessing of a progressive city council to make way for a multi-level parking garage in the inner city, she had died—some said of a broken heart—within a month of relocation to public housing on the city's far south side. (The urban renewal project had continued on schedule in spite of the fact that Doña Luz—always a spirited and independent woman—had, in a last desperate show of defiance, thrown herself down in front of the wrecking ball. This had resulted in a rash of negative publicity and a spate of sympathetic letters that had proved embarrassing to the city fathers. The furor died down within a few weeks, however, as the populace's short-lived attention span turned to more pressing matters like the World Series.)

Within a week of her mother's death, Doña Luz moved out of their one-bedroom apartment at La Reforma. The family heirlooms had been sold over the years to get through the hard times and to supplement Doña Luz's meager earnings as a folder and stacker at Haskell Linen Supply. Doña Luz's remaining tattered possessions—clothing, bedding, an antique trunk, a wood-burning stove, and a few pieces of weather-beaten furniture—had somehow mysteriously and miraculously reappeared in the one section of the abandoned convento ruins that still had a portion of its roof intact. The city fathers, who had annexed the site, chose to look the other way. It was considered an eyesore, used by some as a dump and did not have potential for development in the foreseeable future. They preferred to concentrate their energies and attentions on other more potentially lucrative and respectable areas of the city.

(Doña Luz had been well known to officials before her celebrated encounter with the wrecking ball. She had been, in her more youthful and vigorous days, a thorn in the side of several generations of bureaucrats and attorneys, having laid claim, with faded documents and dog-eared deeds, to several acres of land where the multi-story government complexes now stood in the heart of the city. Needless to say, the Martínez claims proved fruitless in spite of years of wrangling in the courts, their case weakened by the passing of time, the mists of history, a dearth of witnesses and a maze of legal and bureaucratic entanglements.)

Thus the weary city fathers were only too happy to ignore Doña Luz's latest display of obstreperousness, satisfied that age, infirmity and time had taken their toll on her senses. They were wrong, of course, having no way of knowing that Doña Luz's senses were intact, she having abandoned the fleeting awards of politics and protest for what she considered to be more sublime and spiritual matters. Nevertheless, her ghostly comings and goings at the ruins disturbed no one, threatened nothing, and they had received no complaints.

Mi casa es su casa.

Alma hunkered down into the torn plastic of the car seat, closing her eyes and concentrating her thoughts, trying to stay warm. For the air had turned suddenly colder now, and the clouds, gathering speed, had slammed over the weakening sun like a curtain being drawn. Like a room with its candles snuffed out, the orchard and the ruins lay suddenly in shadows. The clouds, blackened and tinged with purple, scudded across the blank sky like so many tall ships in a tempestuous sea.

When Alma at last opened her eyes, she was startled to see Doña Luz standing before her, extending a veined hand to help her rise. Doña Luz had made her way across the bramble-and-branch-strewn field soundlessly, like a ghostly dark cat on padded feet. The old woman's hair was completely white—long and wispy like spun sugar candy. It blew about her face like smoke that threatened to disappear with the quickening wind. She was dressed completely in black: her long dress of coarse homespun cloth hung down to her ankles. The style of the skirt and bodice was reminiscent of those Alma had seen worn by the stern-faced women in the treasured antique photographs of her mother. On her feet Doña Luz wore a pair of old-fashioned hightops with no laces. She wore on her shoulders a threadbare fringed and embroidered shawl of the finest woven silk—the only surviving heirloom of her family's more exalted and prosperous days. Her face was brown, fine-boned and high-cheeked, wrinkled with age and weathered with adversity. Her eyes, set deeply and far apart, were small and bright, and so dark that they seemed to have no pupils. In the sudden obscurity that had come unnaturally with the storm, Doña Luz's luminous eyes were the only beacons in the darkened fields.

"Ven, mi hija. Ya es la hora." Doña Luz addressed Alma in Spanish in an urgent, musical voice. In the many weeks of her vigil, Alma had prepared herself for this moment, and she was not frightened by the sudden apparition of Doña Luz. She grasped Doña Luz's bony arm to steady herself as she arose from her seat; she was surprised at its strength in spite of its weightless fragility. She walked with her silently across the fallow autumn fields to her dwelling place in the convento. The wind was roaring now, whipping the delicate and brittle branches of the fruit trees. The branches, threatening to snap, made a rasping protesting sound that rivaled the din of the wind itself. Before they were halfway across the field, the promised moisture came, not in the usual rain, but in unexpected, silent flakes of snow that fell so thickly that everything in the orchard was blurred as though seen through a cataract-veiled lens. By the time they reached the adobe shelter of Doña Luz, Alma was shivering with the wind and the blowing snow. Doña Luz pushed open the heavy hewn door of her shelter, and in the smoldering half-light of ancient kerosene lamps Alma saw what she thought were hundreds of giant tattered white moths pinned to the ceiling and the rafters and the walls, covering the sparse furniture, or fallen, ankle deep, flightless and abject, on the floor.

"Tú estás encargada de todo esto," Doña Luz whispered to Alma with a dramatic sweep of her hand.

Outside, the snow gathered at the curtainless windows like gauze. . . .

When Alma's eyes had focused and become accustomed to the smoky room, she distinguished through the haze, not moths, but shreds of paper on which notes had been carefully and laboriously written in a spidery scrawl.

Doña Luz continued to explain in a whisper: "This is the history of our people which I have gathered—the land grants and the homesteads and the property transfers; the place-names of the mountains and the rivers and the valleys and the pueblos; the families and their names and their issue; the deeds, honorable and dishonorable; the baptisms, the weddings, the funerals; the prayers and the processions and the santos to whom they are directed; the fiestas, religious and secular; the milagros and the superstitions." She droned on in a cadence, and as she spoke, Alma, still grasping her bony hand and surveying with wonder the testament of Doña Luz, felt the warmth of that hand flow into her being like water being poured. "The recipes, the herbs and the cures; the music and the songs and the dances; the prose and the poems, the sorrows, the joys; the gain and the loss. This is my legacy. But I am old and failing, I entrust it to you lest it be lost and forgotten."

The wind continued to howl and the snow veiled the windows in white lace. . . .

Alma stopped to pick up several pieces of the tattered scraps that lay at her feet, each veined with the faint tracings of Doña Luz's careful script. Squinting in the opaque half-light she read: "On February 10, 1897, Don Jesús María Figueroa perfected the title of his three sections of land under the Homestead Act. He and his family settled in the fertile canyon of the Madrona Draw of the mountain range we call Los Rincones. He named it Rancho de Los Alizos because of the great trees that grew there.

He built his home, corrales and a chapel. There three generations of Figueroas prospered, cultivating grain, vegetables and fruit and raising livestock. In 1939 the United States Department of the Interior, claiming eminent domain, expropriated the land. Before he left for town, the grandson of Don Jesús María Figueroa burned the buildings and the two thousand dollars he received in payment . . ."

Alma read a second note, her eyes straining in the ever-darkening room: "The feast day of San Isidro, the patron saint of farmers, is May 15th. A little statue of the saint is carried through the fields, the farmers and their families singing alabanzas, offering their humble crops and praying that this year's planting might be successful. This is his prayer:

> Señor San Isidro
> De Dios tan querido
> Pues en la labor
> Tu seáis mi padrino
>
> Fuiste a la labor
> Comenzaste a arriar
> Junto con los hombres
> Que iban a sembrar.
>
> Porque sois de Dios amado
> Y adornado de esplandor
> Bendecir nuestro sembrado
> San Isidro Labrador . . ."

And the thickening snow smothered the windows and the ruins like a shroud. . . .

Alma continued to read with a mounting sense of urgency now: "Here is written the corrido of the ill-fated race when Don Antonio Valenzuela lost all he posssessed when his superior and beautiful horse 'El Merino' lost to 'El Pochi' at Los Reales in 1888.

¿Qué hubo, Merino mentado?
¿Qué siente tu corazón?
¿Por qué estás apachangado
  Cuando eres tú en el Tucsón
  El caballo acreditado
  Dueño de la situación . . . ?"

The unfinished song flew from Alma's hands when suddenly, and without warning, a tornadolike gust blew open the unlocked door of Doña Luz's hovel. The airborne flakes blasted in with a ferociousness, and then Alma saw, helpless and aghast, that the shreds of precious paper, in an avalanche of blinding whiteness, had metamorphosed into giant white moths again. They quickened with life and took to the air in a dizzying funnel of flight. Blowing snow mingled with blowing paper and rose and fell and then eddied into a blizzard of memories. And then the memories and the spirit of Doña Luz fluttered out the open door in a thousand swirling fragments in the direction of the south wind somewhere west of Aztlán.

"*No, por favor, damelo,*" Sapito called to him. The man laughed and handed the shell to Sapito, who put his pieces of meat inside it and, with the rest of the boys, wandered back to the river to wait for the paddle boat. The shell was almost too big for him. The boys were all laughing and joking, proud of their accomplishment. They asked Sapito what he was going to do with the shell, but he said that he wasn't sure yet. This wasn't true. Of course, he was already making big, very big, plans for it. . . .

—Alberto Alvaro Ríos, "The Iguana Killer"

THE IGUANA KILLER
Alberto Alvaro Ríos

Alberto Alvaro Ríos, poet and short story writer, is author of numerous books of poetry, including Whispering to Fool the Wind (1982; Walt Whitman Award Winner 1981), Five Indiscretions (1985), and Teodoro Luna's Two Kisses (1990). "The Iguana Killer" is from his award-winning book The Iguana Killer: Twelve Stories of the Heart (1984 Western States Book award in short fiction; reissued 1993). Ríos's fiction has been regularly published in Ploughshares, Story, and the Kenyon Review among other literary journals. He is working on a new book of short stories tentatively entitled Pig Cookies. "The Iguana Killer" is set in Mexico and focuses on a young boy, Sapito, who is an inventor. Though the story is set in Mexico, it represents a very important region for Chicanos: a borderland where cultural transition is an ongoing process. Americans may take for granted the nature of a baseball bat, but a boy like Sapito, who has never seen such a thing, must redefine its purpose within his own cultural context.

Ríos says of his growing up: "I grew up on the border in regards to all kinds of metaphorical borders: in between countries, languages, cultures, decades. In essence, all of this adds up to using binoculars, using two lenses to bring something closer in which you see it better *and understand it more. In which you understand everything has more than one meaning; nothing is static and everything is poetry. You call it fiction, but even fiction has many names for itself. Why even as a poet I can enter that realm."*

SAPITO HAD TURNED EIGHT TWO WEEKS BEFORE AND WAS AT THIS time, living in Villahermosa, the capital city of Tabasco. He had earned his nickname because his eyes bulged to make him look like a frog, and besides, he was the best fly-catcher in all Villa-hermosa. This was when he was five. Now he was eight, but his eyes still bulged and no one called him anything but "Sapito."

Among their many duties, all the boys had to go down to the Rio Grijalva every day and try to sell or trade off whatever homemade things were available and could be carried on these small men's backs. It was also the job of these boys to fish, capture snails, trick tortoises, and kill the iguanas.

Christmas had just passed, and it had been celebrated as usual, very religious with lots of candle smoke and very solemn church masses. There had been no festivities yet, no laughing, but today would be different. Today was the fifth of January, the day the children of Villahermosa wait for all year. Tomorrow would be the *Día de los Reyes Magos*, the Day of the Wise Kings, when presents of all sorts were brought by the Kings and given to friends. Sapito's grandmother, who lived in Nogales in the United States, had sent him two packages. He had seen them, wrapped in blue paper with bearded red clown faces. Sapito's grandmother always sent presents to his family, and she always seemed to know just what Sapito would want, even though they had never met.

That night, Sapito's mother put the packages under the bed where he slept. It was not a cushioned bed, but rather, a ham-mock, made with soft rattan leaves. Huts in Villahermosa were not rented to visitors by the number of rooms, but, instead, by the number of hooks in each place. On these hooks were hung the hammocks of a family. People in this town were born and nursed, then slept and died in these hanging beds. Sapito could remember his grandfather, and how they found him one afternoon after lunch. They had eaten mangoes together. Sapito dreamed about him now, about how his face would turn colors when he told his stories, always too loud.

When Sapito woke up, he found the packages. He played up to his mother, the way she wanted, claiming that the *Reyes* had brought him all these gifts. *Look and look, and look here!* he shouted, but this was probably the last time he would do this, for Sapito was now eight, and he knew better, but did not tell. He opened the two packages from Nogales, finding a baseball and a baseball bat. Sapito held both gifts and smiled, though he wasn't clearly sure what the things were. Sapito had not been born in nor ever visited the United States, and he had no idea what baseball was. He was sure he recognized and admired the ball and knew what it was for. He could certainly use that. But he looked at the baseball bat and was puzzled for some seconds.

It was an iguana-killer. *"¡Mira, mamá! un palo para matar iguanas!"* It was beautiful, a dream. It was perfect. His grandmother always knew what he would like.

In Villahermosa, the jungle was not far from where Sapito lived. It started, in fact, at the end of his backyard. It was not dense there, but one could not walk far before a machete became a third hand, sharper, harder, more valuable than the other two in this other world that sometimes kept people.

This strong jungle life was great fun for a boy like Sapito, who especially enjoyed bringing coconuts out of the tangled vines for his mother. He would look for monkeys in the fat palm trees and throw rocks at them, one after the other. To get back, the monkeys would throw coconuts back at him, yelling terrible monkey-words. This was life before the iguana-killer.

Every day for a week after he had gotten the presents, Sapito would walk about half a mile east along the Río Grijalva with Chachi, his best friend. Then they would cut straight south into the hair of the jungle.

There is a correct way to hunt iguanas, and Sapito had been well-skilled even before the bat came. He and Chachi would look at all the trees until the telltale movement of an iguana was spotted. When one was found, Sapito would sit at the base of the tree, being as quiet as possible, with baseball bat held high and muscles stiff.

The female iguana would come out first. She moved her head around very quickly, almost jerking, in every direction. Sapito knew that she was not the one to kill. She kept the little iguanas in supply—his father had told him. After a few seconds, making sure everything was safe, she would return to the tree and send her husband out, telling him there was nothing to worry about.

The male iguana is always slower. He comes out and moves his head to one side and just stares, motionless, for several minutes. Now Sapito knew that he must take advantage, but very carefully. Iguanas can see in almost all directions at once. Unlike human eyes, both iguana eyes do not have to center in on the same thing. One eye can look forward, and one backward, like a clown, so that they can detect almost any movement. Sapito knew this and was always careful to check both eyes before striking. Squinting his own eyes which always puffed out even more when he was excited, he would not draw back his club. That would waste time. It was already kept high in the air all these minutes. When he was ready, he would send the bat straight down as hard and as fast as he could. Just like that. And if he had done all these things right, he would take his prize home by the tail to skin him for eating that night.

Iguanas were prepared like any other meat, fried, roasted, or boiled, and they tasted like tough chicken no matter which way they were done. In Tabasco, and especially in Villahermosa, iguanas were eaten by everybody all the time, even tourists, so hunting them was very popular. Iguana was an everyday supper, eaten without frowning at such a thing, eating lizard. It was not different from the other things eaten here, the turtle eggs, *cahuamas*, crocodile meat, river snails. And when iguanas were killed, nobody was supposed to feel sad. Everybody's father said so. Sapito did, though, sometimes. Iguanas had puffed eyes like his.

But, if Sapito failed to kill one of these iguanas, he would run away as fast as he could—being sad was the last thing he would think of. Iguanas look mean, they have bloodshot eyes, and people say that they spit blood. Sapito and his friends thought that, since no one they knew had ever been hurt by these monsters, they must not be so bad. This was what the boys thought in town, talking on a summer afternoon, drinking coconuts. But when he missed, Sapito figured that the real reason no one had ever been hurt was that no one ever hung around afterward to find out what happens. Whether iguanas were really dangerous or not, nobody could say for certain. Nobody's parents had ever heard of an iguana hurting anyone, either. The boys went home one day and asked. So, no one worried, sort of, and iguanas were even tamed and kept as pets by the old sailors in Villahermosa, along with the snakes. But only by the sailors.

The thought of missing a hit no longer bothered Sapito, who now began carrying his baseball bat everywhere. His friends were impressed more by this than by anything else, even candy in tin boxes, especially when he began killing four and five iguanas a day. No one could be that good. Soon, not only Chachi, but the rest of the boys began following Sapito around constantly just to watch the scourge of the iguanas in action.

By now, the bat was proven. Sapito was the champion iguana-provider, always holding his now-famous killer-bat. All his friends would come to copy it. They would come every day asking for measurements and questioning him as to its design. Chachi and the rest would then go into the jungle and gather fat, straight roots. With borrowed knives and machetes, they tried to whittle out their own iguana-killers, but failed. Sapito's was machine-made, and perfect.

This went on for about a week, when Sapito had an idea that was to serve him well for a long time. He began renting out the killer-bat for a *centavo* a day. The boys said yes yes right away, and would go out and hunt at least two or three iguanas to make it worth the price, but really, too, so that they could use the bat as much as possible.

For the next few months, the grown-ups of Villahermosa hated Sapito and his bat because all they ate was iguana. But Sapito was proud. No one would make fun of his bulging eyes now.

Sapito was in Nogales in the United States visiting his grandmother for the first time, before going back to Tabasco, and Villahermosa. His family had come from Chiapas on the other side of the republic on a relative-visiting vacation. It was still winter, but no one in Sapito's family had expected it to be cold. They knew about rain, and winter days, but it was always warm in the jungle, even for these things.

Sapito was sitting in front of the house on Sonoita Avenue, on the sidewalk. He was very impressed by many things in this town, especially the streetlights. Imagine lighting up the inside *and* the outside. It would be easy to catch animals at night here. But most of all, he was impressed by his rather large grandmother, whom he already loved very much. He had remembered to thank her for the iguana-killer and the ball. She had laughed and said, *"Por nada, hijo."* As he sat and thought about this, he wrapped the two blankets he had brought outside with him tighter around his small body. Sapito could not understand or explain to himself that the weather was cold and that he had to feel it, everyone did, even him. This was almost an unknown experience to him since he had never been out of the tropics before. The sensation, the feeling of cold, then, was very strange, especially since he wasn't even wet. It was actually hurting him. His muscles felt as if he had held his bat up in the air for an hour waiting for an iguana. Of course, Sapito could have gone inside to get warm near the wood-burning stove, but he didn't like the smoke or the smell of the north. It was a different smell, not the jungle.

So Sapito sat there. Cold had never been important in his life before, and he wasn't going to let it start now. With blankets he could cover himself up and it would surely pass. Covered up for escape, he waited for warmness, pulling the blankets over his head. Sometimes he would put out his foot to see if it was okay yet, the way the lady iguana would come out first.

Then, right then in one fast second, Sapito seemed to feel, with his foot on the outside, a very quiet and strange moment, as if everything had slowed. He felt his eyes bulge when he scrunched up his face to hear better. Something scary caught hold of him, and he began to shiver harder. It was different from just being cold, which was scary enough. His heartbeat was pounding so much that he could feel it in his eyes.

He carefully moved one of the blankets from his face. Sapito saw the sky falling, just like the story his grandmother had told him the first day they had been there. He thought she was joking, or that she didn't realize he was already eight, and didn't believe in such things anymore.

Faster than hitting an iguana Sapito threw his blankets off, crying as he had not cried since he was five and they had nicknamed him and teased him. He ran to the kitchen and grabbed his mother's leg. Crying and shivering, he begged, *"¡Mamá, por favor, perdóneme!"* He kept speaking fast, asking for forgiveness and promising never to do anything wrong in his life ever again. The sky was falling, but he had always prayed, really he had.

His mother looked at him and at first could not laugh. Quietly, she explained that it was *nieve*, snow, that was falling, not the sky. She told him not to be afraid, and that he could go out and play in it, touch it, yes.

Sapito still didn't know exactly what this *nieve* was, but now his mother was laughing and didn't seem worried. In Villahermosa, *nieve* was a good word, it meant ice cream. There was a *nieve* man. Certainly the outside wasn't ice cream, but the white didn't really look bad, he thought, not really. It seemed, in fact, to have great possibilities. Sapito went back outside, sitting again with his blankets, trying to understand. He touched it, and breathed even faster. Then, closing his eyes, which was not easy, he put a little in his mouth.

Sapito's family had been back in Villahermosa for a week now. Today was Sunday. It was the custom here that every Sunday afternoon, since there were no other amusements, the band would play on the *malecón*, an area something like a park by the river, where the boats were all loaded.

Each Sunday it was reserved for this band—that is, the group of citizens that joined together and called themselves a band. It was a favorite time for everyone, as the paddle boat lay resting on the river while its owner played the trumpet and sang loud songs. The instruments were all brass, except for the marimba, which was the only sad sounding instrument. Though it was hit with padded drumsticks, its song was quiet, hidden, always reserved for dusk. Sapito had thought about the marimba as his mother explained about snow. Her voice had its sound for the few minutes she spoke, and held him. Before the marimba, before dusk, however, the brass had full control.

As dusk came, it was time for the *verbenas*, when the girls, young and old, would come in and walk around the park in one direction and the boys would walk the opposite way, all as the marimba played its songs easily, almost by itself. On these Sundays no one was a man or a woman. They were all boys and girls, even the women who always wore black. This was when all the flirting and the smiling of smiles bigger than people's faces took place. Sapito and Chachi and the rest of the smaller boys never paid attention to any of this, except sometimes to make fun of someone's older sister.

An old man, Don Tomasito, the baker, played the tuba. When he blew into the huge mouthpiece, his face would turn purple and his thousand wrinkles would disappear as his skin filled out. Sapito and his friends would choose by throwing fingers, and whoever had the odd number thrown out, matching no one else, was chosen to do the best job of the day. This had become a custom all their own. The chosen one would walk around in front of Don Tomasito as he played, and cut a lemon. Then slowly, very slowly, squeeze it, letting the juice fall to the ground. Don Tomasito's lips would follow.

On this first Sunday afternoon after he had returned, Sapito, after being chased by Señor Saturnino Cantón, who was normally the barber but on Sunday was the policeman, pulled out his prize. Sapito had been preparing his friends all day, and now they were yelling to see this new surprise. This was no iguana-killer, but Sapito hoped it would have the same effect.

Some of the people in Villahermosa used to have photographs of various things. One picture Sapito had particularly remembered. Some ladies of the town, who always made their own clothes, once had a picture taken together. They were a group of maybe ten ladies, in very big dresses and hats, some sitting and some standing. What Sapito recalled now was that they were all barefoot. They were all very serious and probably didn't think of it, but now, Sapito, after traveling to the north and seeing many pictures at his grandmother's house, thought their bare feet were very funny, even if shoes were hard to get and couldn't be made like dresses could. Sapito knew about such things now. He remembered that people in Nogales laughed at him when he was barefoot in the snow.

But now, Sapito had a photograph, too. This was his surprise. Well, what it was, really, was a Christmas card picturing a house with lots of snow around. He had gotten the picture from his grandmother and had taken great care in bringing it back home. He kept the surprise under his shirt wrapped in blue paper against his stomach, so it would stay flat. Here was a picture of the *nieve*, just like he had seen for himself, except there was a lot more of it in the picture. An awful lot more.

At the end of this Sunday, making a big deal with his small hands, he showed this prize to his friends, and told them that *nieve*, which means both snow and ice cream in the Spanish of those who have experienced the two, would fall from the sky in Nogales. Any time at all. His bulging eyes widened to emphasize what he was saying, and he held his bat to be even more convincing.

No one believed him.

"Pues, miren, ¡aquí está!" He showed them the picture, and added now that it was a picture of his grandmother's house, where he had just visited.

When Chachi asked, as Sapito had hoped, if it came down in flavors, he decided that he had gone this far, so why not. *"Vainilla,"* he stated.

As the months went by, so did new stories, and strawberry and pistachio, and he was pretty sure that they believed him. After all, none of them had ever been up north. They didn't know the things Sapito knew. And besides, he still owned the iguana-killer.

Three months after the snow-picture stories had worn off, Señora Casimira, with the help of the town midwife, had a baby girl. The custom here was that mother and baby didn't have to do any work for forty days. No one ever complained. Mostly the little girls would help in the house, doing the errands that were not big enough to bother the boys or the big girls with. They'd throw water out front to quiet the dust. Neighbors would wash the dishes.

For the boys, usually because they could yell louder and didn't want to work with the girls, their job was to go and bring charcoal from the river, to bring bananas and coconuts, and whatever other food was needed. Every morning Sapito and his friends would stand outside the door of Señora Casimira's house, with luck before the girls came, and call in to her, asking if she needed anything. She would tell them yes or no, explaining what to bring if something was necessary.

Spring was here now, and today was Saturday. Sapito thought about this, being wise in the way of seasons now, as he looked down on the Casimira *choza*, the palm-thatched hut in which they lived. Señor Casimira was sure to be there today, he figured. There was no need to hang around, probably. Sapito had saved a little money from renting the killer-bat, and he suggested to his friends that they all go to Puerto Alvarado on the paddle boat. They were hitting him on the back and laughing yes! even before he had finished.

The Río Grijalva comes down from the Sierra Madre mountains, down through the state of Tabasco, through Villahermosa, emptying through Puerto Alvarado several miles north into the Gulf of Mexico. The boys looked over at the Casimira *choza*, then backward at this great river, where the paddle boat was getting ready to make its first trip of the day to Puerto Alvarado. They ran after it, fast enough to leave behind their shadows.

Sapito and his friends had been in Alvarado for about an hour when they learned that a *cahuama*, a giant sea turtle, was nearby. They were on the rough beach, walking toward the north where the rocks become huge. Some palm trees nodded just behind the beach, followed by the jungle, as always. Sometimes Sapito thought it followed him, always moving closer.

Climbing the mossy rocks, Chachi was the one who spotted the *cahuama*. This was strange because the turtles rarely came so close to shore. In Villahermosa, and Puerto Alvarado, the money situation was such that anything the boys saw, like iguanas or the *cahuama*, they tried to capture. They always tried hard to get something for nothing, and here was their chance—

not to mention the adventure involved. They all ran together with the understood intention of dividing up the catch.

They borrowed a rope from the men who were working farther up the shore near the palm trees. *"¡Buena suerte!"* one of the men called, and laughed. Sapito and Chachi jumped in a *cayuco*, a kayak built more like a canoe, which one of the fishermen had left near shore. They paddled out to the floating turtle, jumped out, and managed to get a rope tied around its neck right off. Usually, then, a person had to hop onto the back of the *cahuama* and let it take him down into the water for a little while. Its burst of strength usually went away before the rider drowned or let go. This was the best fun for the boys, and a fairly rare chance, so Sapito, who was closest, jumped on to ride this one. He put up one arm like a tough cowboy. This *cahuama* went nowhere.

The two boys climbed back into the *cayuco* and tried to pull the turtle, but it still wouldn't budge. It had saved its strength, and its strong flippers were more than a match for the two boys now. Everyone on shore swam over to help them after realizing that yells of how to do it better were doing no good. They all grabbed a part of the rope. With pure strength against strength, the six boys sweated, but finally outpulled the stubborn *cahuama*, dragging it onto the shore. It began flopping around on the sand until they managed to tip it onto its back. The turtle seemed to realize that struggling was a waste of its last fat-man energy, and started moving like a slow motion robot, fighting as before but, now, on its back, the flippers and head moved like a movie going too slow.

The *cahuama* had seemed huge as the boys were pulling it, fighting so strong in the water, but it was only about three feet long when they finally took a breath and looked. Yet, they all agreed, this *cahuama* was very fat. It must have been a grandfather.

Chachi went to call one of the grown-ups to help. Each of the boys was sure that he could kill a *cahuama* and prepare it, but this was everybody's, and they wanted it cut right. The men were impressed as the boys explained. The boys were all nervous. Maybe not nervous—not really, just sometimes they were sad when they caught *cahuamas* because they had seen what happens. Like fish, or iguanas, but bigger, and bigger animals are different. Sad, but they couldn't tell anyone, especially not the other boys, or the men. Sapito looked at their catch.

These sailors, or men who used to be sailors, all carried short, heavy machetes, specially made for things taken from the sea. Chachi came back with a man who already had his in hand. The blade was straight because there was no way to shape metal, no anvil in Alvarado. The man looked at Sapito. *"Préstame tu palo,"* he said, looking at Sapito's iguana-killer. Sapito picked it up from where he had left it and handed it to the man, carefully. The fisherman beat the turtle on the head three times fast until it was either dead or unconscious. Then he handed the bat back to Sapito, who was sort of proud, and sort of not.

The man cut the *cahuama's* head off. Some people eat the head and its juice, but Sapito and his friends had been taught not to. No one said anything as it was tossed to the ground. The flippers continued their robot motion.

He cut the side of the turtle, where the underside skin meets the shell. He then pulled a knife out of his pocket, and continued where the machete had first cut, separating the body of the turtle from the shell. As he was cutting he told the boys about the freshwater sac that *cahuamas* have, and how, if they were ever stranded at sea, they could drink it. They had heard the story a hundred times, but nobody knew anybody who really did it. The boys were impatient. Then he separated the underpart from the inside meat, the prize. It looked a little redder than beef. The fins were then cut off—someone would use their leather sometime later.

The man cut the meat into small pieces. The boys took these pieces and washed them in salt water to make the meat last longer. Before cooking them, they would have to be washed again, this time in fresh water to get all the salt off. In the meantime, the salt water would keep the meat from spoiling. One time Sapito forgot, or really he was in too much of a hurry, and he took some *cahuama* home but forgot to tell his mother. It changed colors, and Sapito had to go get some more food, with everybody mad at him. The boys knew that each part of the *cahuama* was valuable, but all they were interested in now was what they could carry. This, of course, was the meat.

The man gave each of the boys some large pieces, and then kept most of it for himself. The boys were young, and could not argue with a grown-up. They were used to this. The fisherman began to throw the shell away.

"No, por favor, damelo," Sapito called to him. The man laughed and handed the shell to Sapito, who put his pieces of meat inside it and, with the rest of the boys, wandered back to the river to wait for the paddle boat. The shell was almost too big for him. The boys were all laughing and joking, proud of their accomplishment. They asked Sapito what he was going to do with the shell, but he said that he wasn't sure yet. This wasn't true. Of course, he was already making big, very big, plans for it.

They got back early in the afternoon, and everyone went home exhausted. Sapito, before going home, went into the jungle and gathered some green branches. He was not very tired yet—he had a new idea, so Sapito spent the rest of the afternoon polishing the shell with sand and the hairy part of some coconuts, which worked just like sandpaper.

When it was polished, he got four of the best branches and whittled them to perfection with his father's knife. Sapito tied these into a rectangle using some *mecate*, something in between rope and string, which his mother had given him. The shell fit halfway down into the opening of the rectangle. It was perfect. Then, onto this frame, he tied two flat, curved branches across the bottom at opposite ends. It moved back and forth like a drunk man. He had made a good, strong crib. It worked, just right for a newborn baby girl.

Sapito had worked hard and fast with the strength of a guilty conscience. Señora Casimira just might have needed something, after all. It was certainly possible that her husband might have had to work today. All the boys had known these facts before they had left, but had looked only at the paddle boat—and it had waved back at them.

Sapito took the crib, hurrying to beat the jungle dusk. Dusk, at an exact moment, even on Sundays, owned the sky and the air in its own strange way. Just after sunset, for about half an hour, the sky blackened more than would be normal for the darkness of early night, and mosquitoes, like pieces of sand, would come up out of the thickest part of the jungle like tornadoes, coming down on the town to take what they could. People always spent this half hour indoors, Sundays, too, even with all the laughing, which stopped then. This was the signal for the marimba's music to take over.

Sapito reached the *choza* as the first buzzings were starting. He listened at the Casimiras' door, hearing the baby cry like all babies. The cradle would help. He put it down in front of the wooden door without making any noise, and knocked. Then, as fast as he could, faster than that even, he ran back over the hill, out of sight. He did not turn around. Señora Casimira would find out who had made it. And he would be famous again, thought Sapito, famous like the other times. He felt for the iguana-killer that had been dragging behind him, tied to his belt, and put it over his right shoulder. His face was not strong enough to keep away the smile that pulled his mouth, his fat eyes all the while puffing out.

On the way to Little Feo's house, which was only three blocks from my own, I saw Doña Toña walking towards me. When she was close enough to hear me, I began to speak but she cut me off, saying that she knew my mother was sick and had asked for her. I got a little scared because there was no way that she could have known that my mother had asked for her, yet she knew. My head was bombarded with thoughts that perhaps she might be a witch after all. . . .

—Louie The Foot González, "Doña Toña of Nineteenth Street"

DOÑA TOÑA
OF NINETEENTH STREET

Louie The Foot González

Louie The Foot González *is an artist and writer who has conducted community workshops throughout the United States, including Chicago, New Mexico, San Jose, Los Angeles, and Delano. A recognized master of the silkscreen process, through his poster art he has promoted the political goals of the Chicano Movement and brought together members of the community—most especially "kids and their families" during the workshops he conducts year-round throughout the country.*

González's "Doña Toña of Nineteenth Street" employs the figure of the curandera, *a woman of faith in herbs rather than commercial medicines, a shamanistic wise woman whose origins are in the indigenous culture. For the believer, a curandera's healing powers far surpass those of modern medicine. The* curandera's *act of healing arises from her faith in the larger forces of life: the plants, the earth, and the spirits. Though she is a revered and respected member of the community, the* curandera *is also feared. González says of this part of his growing up: "This story is based on a character that lived a few houses down from me in Sacramento in our predominantly Mexican neighborhood where I grew up pretty much speaking Spanish to my family and neighbors. The modern world couldn't really help us due to language differences, so we had*

*to help ourselves. We relied on Doña Toña to help us in the
neighborhood—this was in 1958–1960 that she's in my mind. The
things she did always seemed to work; though they were sometimes
strange, they were always magical. And this made me think more
about my parents' heritage, such as my mother's involvement in the
movement. This gave me the courage to make my voice more vocal
and my thinking more political. I got to meet a lot of the leaders,
such as César Chávez, on the picket lines, where I began to jot
down things that bothered me, that gave me encouragement. And I
began to draw these pictures with words and to incorporate my
experiences with bilingualism, my home being both English and
Spanish."*

HER NAME WAS DOÑA TOÑA AND I CAN'T HELP BUT REMEMBER THE
fear I had of the old lady. Maybe it was the way all the younger
kids talked about her:

"Ya, man. I saw her out one night and she was pulling some
weeds near the railroad tracks and her cat was meowing away
like it was ready to fight that big black dog and, man, she looked
just like a witch, like the Llorona trying to dig up her children."

"Martin's tellin' everybody that she was dancin' aroun' real
slow and singin' some witch songs in her backyard when it was
dark and everybody was asleep."

Doña Toña was always walking somewhere . . . anywhere . . .
even when she had no particular place to go. When she walked,
it was as though she were making a great effort because her
right leg was kind of funny. It dragged a little and it made her
look as if her foot were made of solid metal.

Her face was the color of lightly creamed coffee. The wrinkles
around her forehead and eyes were like the rings of a very old
tree. They gave her age as being somewhere around seventy-

five years old, but as I was to discover later, she was really eighty-nine. Even though her eyes attracted much attention, they always gave way to her mouth. Most of the people that I had observed looking at her directed their gaze at her mouth. Doña Toña had only one tooth to her name and it was the strangest tooth I had ever seen. It was exceptionally long and it stuck out from her upper gum at a forty-five degree angle. What made it even stranger was that it was also twisted. She at one time probably had an overabundance of teeth, until they began to push against each other, twisting themselves, until she had only one last tooth left. It was the toughest of them all, the king of the hill, 'el mero chingón.'

Doña Toña was born in 1885 in one of the innumerable little towns of México. The Mexican Revolution of 1910 drove her from her little-town home when she was twenty-seven years old. She escaped the mass bloodshed of the Revolution by crossing the border into the United States and living in countless towns from Los Angeles to Sacramento, where she became the most familiar sight in Barrio Cinco. She was one of the barrio's landmarks; when you saw her, you knew that you were in the barrio. She had been there longer than anyone else and yet no one, except perhaps her daughter María, knew very much about her. Some people said that was the way she wanted it. But as far as I could see, she didn't show signs of wanting to be alone.

Whenever Doña Toña caught someone watching her during one of her never-ending strolls, she would stop walking and look at that person head-on. No one could keep staring at her once she had started to stare back. There was something in Doña Toña's stare that could make anybody feel like a child. Her crow-black eyes could hypnotize almost anybody. She could have probably put an owl to sleep with her stare.

★ ★ ★

Doña Toña was Little Feo's grandmother. She lived with her daughter, María, who was Little Feo's mother. All of Little Feo's ten years of life had passed without the outward lovingness that grandmothers are supposed to show. But the reason for it was Little Feo's own choice.

Whenever Little Feo, who was smaller, thinner, and darker than the rest of the barrio ten years olds, was running around with us (Danny, Fat Charlie, Bighead, Joe Nuts, and a few other guys that lived close by) nobody would say anything about his "abuelita." Before, whenever anybody used to make fun of her or use her for the punchline of a joke, Little Feo would get very quiet; his fists would begin to tighten and his face would turn a darker shade as all his blood rushed to his brain. One time when Fat Charlie said something like, "What's black and flies at night? Why . . . it's Feo's granny," Little Feo pounced on him faster than I had ever seen anybody pounce on someone before. Fat Charlie kicked the hell out of Little Feo, but he never cracked another joke like that again, at least not about Doña Toña.

Doña Toña was not taken very seriously by very many people until someone in the barrio got sick. Visits to Doctor Herida when someone got sick were common even though few people liked to go to him because he would just look at the patient and then scribble something on a prescription form and tell the sick one to take it next door to McAnaws Pharmacy to have it filled. Herida and the pharmacist had a racket going. When the medicine Herida prescribed didn't have the desired effect, the word was sent out in the barrio that Doña Toña was needed somewhere. Sometimes it was at the Osorio house, where Jaime was having trouble breathing, or the Canaguas place, where what's-her-name was gaining a lot of weight. Regardless of the illness, Doña Toña would always show up, even if she had to drag herself across the barrio to get to where she was needed; and, many times, that's exactly what she did. Once at the place of need, she did whatever it was she had to and then she left, asking nothing of anyone. Usually, within a short time of her visit—hours (if the illness were a natural one) or a day or two (if it were supernatural)—the patient would show signs of improvement.

Doña Toña was never bothered about not receiving any credit for her efforts.

"You see, comadre, I tol' you the medicina would estar' to work."

"Ándale, didn't I tell you that Doctor Herida knew what he was doing?"

"I didn't know what that stupid old lady thought she was going to accomplish by doing all the hocus-pocus with those useless herbs and plants of hers. Everybody knows that an old witch's magic is no match for a doctor's medicine. That crazy old WITCH."

And that's how it was. Doña Toña didn't seem to mind that they called on her to help them and, after she had done what she could, they proceeded to badmouth her. But that's the way it was and she didn't seem to mind.

I remember, perhaps best of all, the time my mother got sick. She was very pale and her whole body was sore. She went to see Doctor Herida and all he did was ask *her* what was wrong and, without even examining her, he prescribed something that she bought at McAnaws. When all the little blue pills were gone, the soreness of her bones and the paleness of her skin remained. Not wanting to go back to Herida's, my mother asked me to go get Doña Toña. I would have never gone to get the old lady, but I had never before seen my mother so sick. So I went.

On the way to Little Feo's house, which was only three blocks from my own, I saw Doña Toña walking towards me. When she was close enough to hear me, I began to speak but she cut me off, saying that she knew my mother was sick and had asked for her. I got a little scared because there was no way that she could have known that my mother had asked for her, yet she knew. My head was bombarded with thoughts that perhaps she might be a witch after all. I had the urge to run away from her but I didn't. I began to think that if she were a witch, why was she always helping people? Witches were bad people. And Doña Toña wasn't. It was at this point that my fear of her disappeared and, in its place, sprouted an intense curiosity.

Doña Toña and I reached my house and we climbed the ten steps that led to the front door. I opened the door and waited for her to step in first, but she motioned with her hand to me to lead the way.

Doña Toña looked like a little moving shadow as we walked through the narrow hallway that ended at my mother's room. Her leg dragged across the old faded linoleum floor making a dull scraping sound. I reached the room and opened the door. My mother was half-asleep on the bed as Doña Toña entered. I walked in after her because I wanted to see what kind of magic she was going to have to perform in order to save my mother; but as soon as Doña Toña began taking some candles from her sack, my mother looked at me and told me to go outside to play with the other kids.

I left the room but had no intentions of going outside to play. My mother's bedroom was next to the bathroom and there was a door that connected both of them. The bathroom could be locked only from the inside, so my mother usually left it un-locked in case some unexpected emergency came up. I went into the bathroom and, without turning on the light, looked through the crack of the slightly open door.

My mother was sprawled on the bed, face down. Her night gown was open exposing her shoulder blades and back. Doña Toña melted the bottoms of two candles and then placed one between the shoulder blades and the other at the base of the spine. Doña Toña began to pray as she pinched the area around the candles. Her movements were almost imperceptible. The candlelight made her old brown hands shine and her eyes looked like little moons. Doña Toña's voice got louder as her hands moved faster across my mother's back. The words she prayed were indecipherable even with the increase in volume. The scene reminded me of a priest praying in Latin during Mass, asking God to save us from damnation while no one knew what he was saying. The wax from the candles slid down onto my mother's back and shoulder blades, forming what looked like roots. It looked as though there were two trees of wax growing out of her back.

About a half an hour went by before the candles had burned themselves into oblivion, spreading wax all over my mother's back. Doña Toña stopped praying and scraped the wax away. She reached into the sack and pulled out a little baby food jar half-filled with something that resembled lard. She scooped some of the stuff out with her hand and rubbed it over the areas that had been covered by the wax. Next, she took from the sack a coffee can filled with an herb that looked like oregano. She sprinkled the herb over the lardlike substance and began rubbing it into the skin.

When she was almost finished, Doña Toña looked around the room and stared straight into the dark opening of the bathroom. I felt that she knew I was behind the door but I stayed there anyway. She turned back to face my mother, bent down, and whispered something in her ear.

Doña Toña picked up all her paraphernalia and returned it to its place in the sack. As she started to leave, she headed for the bathroom door. The heart in my chest almost exploded before I heard my mother's voice tell Doña Toña that she was leaving through the wrong door.

I hurried from the bathroom and ran through the other rooms in the house so that I could catch Doña Toña to show her the way out. I reached her as she was closing the door to my mother's room and led her to the front of the house. As she was making her way down the stairs I heard her mumble something about "learning the secrets" then she looked up at me and smiled. I couldn't help but smile back because her face looked like a brown jack-o-lantern with only one strange tooth carved into it. Doña Toña turned to walk down the remaining four stairs. I was going to ask her what she had said, but by the time I had the words formed in my mind, she had reached the street and was on her way home.

I went back inside the house and looked in on my mother. She was asleep. I knew that she was going to be all right and that it was not going to be because the "medicina" was beginning to work or because Doctor Herida knew what he was doing.

In the great hall, with the sunlight arching across the marble walls, Juana Inés glued her gaze to the Vicereine's eyes and pleaded silently to be taken in, to be saved from the ignorance of the Matas. The Viceroy twirled the ends of his thin mustache, his eyebrows raised as he studied Juana Inés's face.

"You say she taught herself Latin?" the Viceroy asked her uncle.

"And many other subjects as well, your Excellency. Juanita is a most studious girl. She impresses all of our friends with her conversation. Of course, we don't really understand why . . ."

—Alicia Gaspar de Alba, "Juana Inés"

JUANA INÉS

Alicia Gaspar de Alba

Alicia Gaspar de Alba *has been published in journals and anthologies, including* New Chicana/Chicano Writing, Blue Mesa Review, *and* Massachusetts Review. *She is the author of a collection of poetry,* Beggar on the Cordoba Bridge *(1989) and of a forthcoming volume of short fiction,* The Mystery of Survival and Other Stories *(1993). She is completing her Ph.D. in American Studies at the University of New Mexico, and is currently a Chicana Dissertation Fellow at the University of California at Santa Barbara. "Juana Inés" examines the childhood of Sor Juana Inés de la Cruz (circa 1650–1690), an important literary figure in Chicana/o history who was the first woman openly to question male domination as taught by the Catholic Church. She entered a convent and by age eight was writing plays and poetry. Women were not allowed advanced study. However, her mother cut Sor Juana's hair short and dressed her in boys' clothing so that she could continue her studies. This story gives us a glimpse into the life of Chicanas in their struggles in a society whose traditions often function to limit the accomplishments of women.*

The author says of her youth: "I did not, technically speaking, 'grow up Chicana,' because it was drilled into me by my Mexican immigrant family that I was a Mexicana, and that Chicanos were

*an embarrassment to our race. What was wrong with Chicanos,
according to my family, was their language—the way they 'ruined'
the Spanish tongue by mixing it with English—and their
assimilation into the 'American' way of life, which meant their
rejection of Mexican beliefs, values, and customs. Thus, I grew up
oppressing my own gente, feeling superior because I could speak
both English and Spanish without switching back and forth, and
because I resisted Americanization and proudly affirmed my
Mexican identity. Not until my junior year in college did I learn,
through a Chicano literature course that made me aware for the first
time of my own cultural schizophrenia (or identity crisis), that I
was, indeed, a Chicana, and that internalized oppression is part of
the colonized condition. The story that follows relates to me
autobiographically on another level, another identity crisis. It speaks
to the fear and self-inflicted torture, the shame and confusion, that a
teenage girl coming to terms with her lesbianism experiences in a
rigidly homophobic world. Thus, the protagonist's repression of her
lesbian desire coincides with my own, and is also symbolic of the
repression of my Chicana identity in a staunchly nationalistic
family."*

BLESS ME, PADRE, FOR I HAVE SINNED; MY LAST CONFESSION WAS
*on All Soul's Day. Forgive me for not going to the confessional, but
I couldn't speak this sin out loud, Padre, and I may not, may never,
be able to speak it in writing. Punish me, Padre, as you would punish
the vilest sinner, but don't make me say this to you. Pull out my
tongue, Padre, poke out my eyes, lock me up in a convent. Do what
you will, just don't make me speak. I beseech the most pure, the most
benevolent, our Lady of Guadalupe, to save me from this ugliness.
Hide me under your robe, dear Lady, crush me under your feet like a
serpent.*

"Open this door, Juana Inés, or I shall have one of the masons
take it down," said la Marquesa from the other side of the

barricaded door. "What is the matter with you, girl? Do you have the pox that you quarantine yourself in this way?"

But Juana Inés could not answer. She dropped the quill on the parchment and felt the ugliness swell within her, spilling out of her eyes like innocent tears.

"I understand that you must be afraid, Juana," called la Marquesa. "But the Viceroy and the professors are waiting for you in the hall. You don't want to shame the palace, do you?"

If only you knew about me, thought Juana Inés, about this love, this sin I cannot confess. But la Marquesa was right. If she refused to participate in the tournament, the palace would be put to shame, and she could not let her ugliness contaminate the Viceroy's plans.

"I have an outstanding idea, Señora," the Viceroy had announced to his wife one evening over churros and hot chocolate. "The palace is going to sponsor a tournament between our brilliant Juana Inés and the most erudite members of the university. I'll call together professors from every field—theology, music, poetry, philosophy, mathematics, even astronomy—and we'll challenge them to find a gap in Juana Inés's education."

"But I'm only eighteen, your grace," Juana Inés had tried to dissuade him, "and nothing but a lady-in-waiting. Surely I have not learned enough to participate in such a contest."

"Nonsense," the Viceroy had said. "If you can answer their questions the way you play chess, I am certain that you will astonish and outwit them all. Don't be modest, Juana Inés; I can't abide modesty in an intellect like yours."

Again, la Marquesa ordered her page to pound on Juana Inés's door.

"Yes, my lady," Juana Inés answered la Marquesa's entreaties at last, "I am on my way."

"Thank God you have recovered your senses, girl. Do hurry. The professors are already finished with their dinner. I'm afraid you won't have time to eat, Juana."

"I'm not hungry, my lady," called Juana Inés, holding the confession she had just written over the flame of a candle. She opened her wardrobe and gazed at her fine gowns, all gifts from la Marquesa, but she could not wear anything that would stimulate the ugliness and distract her. In this contest, the only thing that mattered was her memory; her body and face were inconsequential, and so she would wear the plainest gown, the black one with the white lace collar and the ivory buttons.

In the mirror, her eyes looked as though she had rubbed them with prickly pears, and her skin was the color of maguey pulp. She poured water into the basin and wet her hair. She would braid it simply, with a black ribbon and would wear no jewelry, not even the cameo that her mother had sent her when she came to live at the palace, and certainly not the earrings or the necklace that la Marquesa had given her for her seventeenth birthday. She pushed the heavy bureau away from the door, expecting la Marquesa's page to be waiting for her, but the gallery was empty except for slave girls draping cloths over the bird cages.

Inhaling and exhaling slowly to loosen the muscles in her throat, Juana Inés walked to the great hall where the contest was to be held, thinking not of the questions that would be put to her—deep in her mind, she knew that the Viceroy's faith in her intellect was not unfounded—but of the first time she had performed in the great hall, the first time she had laid eyes on Leonor Carreto, Marquesa de Mancera.

"The Viceroy has summoned Juana Inés to the palace!" her uncle nearly shouted. "Listen to this, María: 'Esteemed don Juan de Mata: the Vicereine, la Marquesa de Mancera, requests the honor of making your niece's acquaintance. The court is anxious to meet the girl scholar who is stirring the talk of Mexico City.' "

"Oh my God," said her aunt María.

It was true that Juana Inés had been studying ever since she was three, that she had taught herself Latin grammar, geometry, and astronomy, that she had studied Greek philosophy and Roman law, but she did not consider herself a scholar, much less a prodigy as some chose to call her to the utter horror of her guardians who daily expected the Inquisition to accuse them of harboring a heretic in their midst. But the gossip flowed from the servants, and the city buzzed with the novelty of a girl who could read the constellations as easily as music.

"It's unnatural for a girl to know as much as you do, Juana Inés," her aunt had often admonished her. "You should learn how to embroider, how to crochet, like your cousins; those are safe things for girls to know."

Juana Inés did not argue with the Matas, but she knew that her wits would not be threaded through the eye of a needle. Her mind was the very pattern that the needle and thread tried to follow, the very fabric without which the pattern would be useless.

On the day of the Viceroy's summons, her aunt altered one of her own silk dresses for Juana Inés, and packed a trunk with Juana Inés's things just in case the Viceroy intended to offer her a position at the palace. The following morning, her uncle escorted Juana Inés to the court in his finest carriage. Juana Inés was sixteen. She had survived the ridicule and torment of the Matas for eight years. The idea of living at court, even if just to scrub the floors of the palace, was like a miracle to her. Surely there would be a library of exceptional quality at the court. Surely the Viceroy would not fear the Inquisition.

In the great hall, with the sunlight arching across the marble walls, Juana Inés glued her gaze to the Vicereine's eyes and pleaded silently to be taken in, to be saved from the ignorance of the Matas. The Viceroy twirled the ends of his thin mustache, his eyebrows raised as he studied Juana Inés's face.

"You say she taught herself Latin?" the Viceroy asked her uncle.

"And many other subjects as well, your Excellency. Juanita is a most studious girl. She impresses all of our friends with her conversation. Of course, we don't really understand why . . ."

"Does she play any musical instruments?" the Viceroy interrupted.

"Oh, she's quite a musician, your Excellency. She's an expert on the mandolin *and* the vihuela. She doesn't know much about sewing . . ."

Juana Inés's fingers had turned to wood. She knew what was coming next.

"We must have a demonstration," the Viceroy said, and snapped his fingers to the page standing at his side.

"Bring a mandolin from the music room," the Viceroy ordered. "Quickly."

The page bowed and scurried from the hall. Her uncle continued to extol her virtues as a musician but Juana Inés hardly heard him in her anxiety. She was trying to determine what would be the most appropriate thing to play. The piece had to be both modest and original, but it needed to live up to her uncle's praises, and so had to be . . . what was the best way to describe it? . . . haunting. She had to play the most haunting, most delicate piece she had ever written.

The Vicereine smiled at Juana Inés, leisurely fanning herself with a Chinese dragon.

"What will you play for us, Doña Ramírez de Asbaje?" the Viceroy asked Juana Inés.

"I would like to play one of my own compositions, if your majesties have no objection." The meekness in her voice surprised Juana Inés.

"No objections at all, my dear," the Vicereine spoke at last. "Does your composition have a name?"

The page scurried back into the hall.

"Hand it to the young lady," the Viceroy instructed the page. Juana Inés took the mandolin and fit the mahogany-and-spruce-striped belly of the instrument to her body, unable to resist caressing the sleek rose face. Inhaling the scent of the virgin wood, she tuned the strings, aware of the significance of this performance, aware of the Vicereine's eyes, of the jeweled buckles on the Viceroy's shoes, of her uncle's nervous breathing.

"Juanita, the Marquesa asked you the name of this composition?" her uncle said.

Juana Inés raised her head and looked at the Vicereine. "I call it 'The Cell,' my lady. That's the name of the room where I was born in my grandfather's hacienda."

"How very bizarre," said the Vicereine.

Juana Inés filled the sacks of her lungs with air. With her left hand she clasped the neck of the mandolin. With her right she removed the plectrum from between the strings and started to play. She had written the piece in the dark morning of her fifteenth birthday, upon awakening from a dream: Her grandfather stood on a riverbank in a circle of light, leaning against a bishop's crook. To reach him, Juana Inés had to float across the river on her back, arms over her head, but when she reached the light, it was a woman—not her mother or either of her sisters—a strange woman waiting on the riverbank, holding a black shawl. "Where's my abuelo?" Juana Inés asked. The woman said, "Don't be afraid. You're safe now."

When she awakened from the dream, she could hear this music in her head. The notes carried the delicacy of baptism and the mystery of death, and so she had called it 'The Cell.' Her mother had given birth to her in that room, and eight years later her grandfather had died there.

Juana Inés plucked the last few notes, then set the instrument down on her lap and kept her eyes on the Vicereine's face.

"Excelentísimo," said the Viceroy, tapping the fingers of one hand into the palm of the other. Beside him, the Vicereine stared at Juana Inés in a way that she could not decipher, a way that made her heart beat with a question that she had no words for.

"We have heard that you are quite a conversationalist," the Viceroy was saying to her, "that you can talk about any subject put to you. Is that true?"

Juana Inés said to the Viceroy: "I doubt I know as much as you, your Excellency; I am a girl, after all, and have not had the benefit of a formal education. I have read quite a few books, I guess. I have a good memory."

"If this girl had her choice between eating and reading, she would be a skeleton by now," said her uncle. "Why, she even renounced cheese . . ."

"She will not have to make that choice here," the Viceroy replied, smiling at Juana Inés under the tails of his mustache. "Would you like to stay at the palace, Juana Inés, and be a lady-in-waiting to la Marquesa?"

"Sir, I would be a slave to la Marquesa," Juana Inés answered, the relief in her voice thick as powder.

"Well, Señora Marquesa," the Viceroy turned to his wife. "Do you have an opinion to offer?"

"I believe you have made a wise decision, Husband," said the Vicereine, closing her fan and tilting her head to one side as if to study Juana Inés from a different angle. "I am sure Juana Inés will be quite an inspiration to me."

Juana Inés looked down and tried to keep her chin from shaking, but she could not control the tears of gratitude that streaked her face and slipped through the strings of the mandolin.

"And *I* believe the girl is baptizing the mandolin," said the Viceroy, chuckling. Juana Inés jumped up and tried to dry the instrument with her silk sleeve.

"Never mind," the Viceroy told her. "It's yours, to continue enchanting la Marquesa."

The chamberlain and his assistant were serving cups of hot chocolate to the professors and the guests seated in the great hall. The noblest hidalgos and their families had been invited to witness the contest, and among them sat Padre Antonio, the court's father confessor and spiritual adviser, the kind of prist who, it was rumored, knelt to the whip as passionately as to the cross and stained the walls of his quarters with his own blood. Juana Inés felt exposed. Surely the ugliness in her soul would be apparent to Padre Antonio. For an instant, she felt her memory and everything she had learned and stored inside it evaporate in the heat of her fear.

"There you are, Juana Inés!" said the Viceroy, getting to his feet as she entered the hall. "Gentlemen, it is my supreme pleasure to introduce you to the court's protégée, the Vicereine's friend and companion, Doña Juana Inés Ramírez de Asbaje."

Juana Inés stood beside the bench that had been placed in front of the audience and curtsied. "Forgive me for keeping you waiting; I have not been well," she said, her voice trembling.

"Should we postpone the tournament, Juana?" asked the Viceroy.

"I would not want the professors to think that I am surrendering without a struggle," she answered, sitting down. "I am quite ready to begin, thank you, Sir."

"Very well," said the Viceroy, turning to face the audience. "Esteemed ladies, noble gentlemen, as you know, we are here to test our protégée's education, which, as you also know, she has gained without the aid or direction of teachers. We shall see if our dignified professors can find a gap in Juana Inés's education, or, indeed, if Juana Inés will find a gap in theirs."

One of the professors in the audience guffawed into the velvet puff of his sleeve.

"Señor López," said the Viceroy. "Since you are in such a sanguine humor today, I will give *you* the honor of asking the first question."

Juana Inés avoided the green light of the Vicereine's eyes but looked straight into Padre Antonio's line of vision to ascertain whether or not he knew about her secret. The priest nodded at her paternally, and Juana Inés felt her fear dissolve and her memory stir back to life. She knew that the paleness of her face and her red-rimmed eyes and her quivering voice betrayed her, made her seem the vapid, frightened girl whom the professors had come to patronize or to embarrass. But she was determined to win this contest; if she could only keep her logic intact and not feel like a monkey performing in the Plaza Mayor, her victory was certain.

"Doña Ramírez," the professor named López commenced, "I would be most honored to hear from your learned lips the five conditions of the solitary bird, according to San Juan de la Cruz."

Juana Inés closed her eyes and concentrated on the image of her diary, saw her hand copying out the very text that Professor López was now asking her to repeat.

"He must fly to the highest peak; he must not be afraid of solitude; he must sing to the sky; his color must not be definitive; his song must be very soft. And I will add, Sir, though you didn't ask me to expound upon this symbol, that San Juan de la Cruz was talking about the human soul. I recorded the passage in my diary because it was the first time I had ever come across an idea that made me weep, and weeping, Sir, is not my nature."

"What do you say, Señor López?" asked the Viceroy. "Has she satisfied your curiosity?"

The professor pressed his lips together and nodded reluctantly. "I acknowledge your astute assessment of the girl's memory, Excellency," he murmured.

"Next!" called the Viceroy.

An older professor with a long wig stood up.

"Ah, Don Jorge," said the Viceroy. "I trust your question will prove somewhat more of a challenge to our protégée than the last one."

"Once upon a time," the old man spoke, his voice like a bullfrog's croak, "the art of poetry along with all the other arts was considered nothing more than imitation, artifices that imitated the one true art. What can you tell us about that, young lady?"

The contest allowed Juana Inés to confirm what she had always suspected of her mind: it was divided into two diametrically opposite halves. While she exercised the side that contained the knowledge she had gleaned from her studies to answer the professors' questions, in the other half of her mind, she was imagining the confession that she would never be able to make to Padre Antonio.

Bless me, Father, for I have sinned a deep and horrible sin, the blackest sin.

"If you would be so kind, Doña Ramírez, as to construct a syllogism for us, please."

There is love in my heart, Father, but it is a vile love, an unnatural, unnameable love, and yet, so deep, so pure.

"Have you any scholastic, or even scientific, evidence, Doña Ramírez, for this quaint conjecture of yours that women can aspire to the same mental and spiritual dimensions as men?"

I have violated the Vicereine's kindness, Father. I have sullied her with my ugliness.

"Perhaps our illustrious audience would enjoy listening to you recite a passage from *Don Quixote*, Doña Ramírez? I had in mind the old knight's monologue upon his strange enchantment."

I help her bathe. I braid her hair. I pour her chocolate. I wait on her, as I am supposed to do, Father, as her other ladies do. But none of them, I know, are tainted as I am. They grumble among themselves about how willful she is, how bad-tempered she is, how she treats them no better than slaves.

"Doña Ramírez, would you define mathematics for us, please, and explain Euclid's contribution to the field as well as the Archimedean principle?"

I know they're right, Father, but I don't blame her. She's an artist trapped in a woman's body; I understand her. I love her.

"You were speaking earlier of the nature of light and spiritual illumination, Doña Ramírez. Let us now examine the subject of light in a less esoteric, more mundane manner. I am alluding, of course, to the sun and will ask you, specifically, albeit circumlocutiously, about Copernicus. What theory did Copernicus propose that caused such an uproar in the Holy Office?"

I was not always aware of how I felt, Father. It came upon me last week, while we were . . . while I was . . . we were in the garden. La Marquesa was doing a sketch she wanted to call "Athena Among Calla Lilies," and she had me posing for her in a yellow sheet fashioned to resemble a Greek tunic. She had snapped a calla off its stem and tucked it behind my ear, and I suggested to her that, as the patroness of war, Athena would probably not wear flowers in her hair. I tried to convince her to change the title of the sketch to "Aphrodite Among Calla Lilies," but she laughed at my suggestion. That would lack originality, Juana Inés, she said. Everyone expects the goddess of love to be surrounded by flowers, not the goddess of wisdom and patroness of war. I want to depict Athena as she might have been without the armor, a lithe, carefree, voluptuous Athena, unburdened by thoughts of war, innocent yet succulent, like the callas.

"Doña Ramírez, how would you explain the influence of the zodiac on a person's character and destiny?"

And then her Excellency made a comment about the color yellow, about how it set off the hazel flecks in my eyes and removed the melancholic pallor of my skin. I never noticed what an expressive mouth you have, Juana Inés, la Marquesa said, and my knees buckled, Father. I don't know, it may have been la Marquesa's unusual description of the lilies that disarmed me, that made me so susceptible to the sound of her voice, or perhaps the sun had been beating on my head too long (we *had* been out there all morning), but I started to feel very confused. I felt an attack of vertigo coming on, and my whole body itched as though I had just been attacked by a swarm of bees. I had to sit down. Her Excellency was most alarmed; she blamed herself for causing me what she interpreted as sunstroke, and immediately called one of the maids to bring a fan and a pitcher of water. She had me move to the grape arbor where it was cool and shady, and she actually fanned me, herself, crooning to me as though I were her own daughter. But it was not a daughterly feeling that I was feeling, Father. And it was not a daughterly instinct that made me lay my head on her breast and intoxicate myself with her closeness. Father, I'm so ashamed. So frightened. I love her so much.

"I didn't quite hear that, Doña Ramírez?"

"Forgive me, Sir," said Juana Inés, realizing that she had wandered too far into that dangerous hemisphere of her mind where logic had no roots. "Would you repeat the question, please? I suppose I'm getting rather tired."

"Of course you are, my dear," said the Vicereine. Turning to the Viceroy, she added, "Perhaps, Husband, we have seen enough. I, myself, am convinced that what I have witnessed here today is the equivalent of a royal galleon fending off the bothersome arrows of a few canoes."

"Yes, Madam, an exquisite analogy," said the Viceroy, "but I should like to hear our galleon's response to that last question. Do proceed, Professor de la Cadena."

"I was asking our girl scholar if she had any idea what the letter O symbolized to that very advanced, though admittedly pagan, culture of the Mayan people?" said the professor, who had gotten to his feet and stood with his fists at his waist, staring at Juana Inés with a palpable disdain.

"As you know, Sir, there is not much written about the history and philosophy of ancient México," said Juana Inés, "but in my grandfather's hacienda where I grew up, there was an old Mayan gardener who told me a story about three sacred letters; I believe they were the T, the G, and the O. She was a very old woman and I a very young girl, starving for stories. Unfortunately, all I remember of that story is this: once upon a time, there was a great and blessed tree known as the Tree of Life that grew as high as the Milky Way, the spiral path through which the gods traveled, through which existence unfolded, and the fruit of this tree was the human mind, ripe and round as a pomegranate, its seeds filled with what she called The Nothing and The Everything."

"Enough of this pagan chattering!" a voice called out. It was Padre Antonio, who was now also on his feet behind the Viceroy and la Marquesa, his face white as bone. "The zodiac! The tree of life! The spiral path! I'm shocked, your Excellency, that you have permitted this girl to spice her studies with arcane reading!"

"Scandalous!" said Professor de la Cadena.

"A royal galleon, indeed!" the Viceroy said, applauding. The rest of the audience followed suit, but Juana Inés could sense that the air between their palms had become as taut as her own vocal chords.

"We have a guitar trio waiting in the patio, everybody," announced the Vicereine.

Pretending to ignore their shifty glances and shaking heads, Juana Inés watched them—the murmuring señoras, the indignant caballeros—follow la Marquesa through the glass doors of the salon. She had expected la Marquesa to felicitate her in some way: a kiss, an embrace, even a smile. But she had not so much as looked at Juana Inés, and Juana Inés felt paralyzed on her bench, abandoned. Two meters away the Viceroy and Padre Antonio were arguing about her education.

"How can she know if something is forbidden when she has no teachers?" the Viceroy asked.

"As censor for the Holy Office, your Excellency, I must report the girl. Her soul is in danger of excommunication if she continues with these heretical studies."

"Let us be reasonable, Padre Antonio. You have known for as long as the girl has lived at the palace that she is an omnivore of books and that she has mnemonic capacities of magnanimous proportions. Is it her fault that she remembers things she shouldn't? Will the Holy See excommunicate a young girl for having a good memory?"

"Joan of Arc was roasted at the stake for listening to angels," said Padre Antonio, "and she was the same age as Juana Inés."

The black magnet of Padre Antonio's eyes pulled Juana Inés's gaze away from the lace collar of her dress.

"Look at her, your Excellency," said the priest. "She knows she has wronged God and our Mother Church, do you not, Juana Inés? Come here, Child. We must speak of the future of your soul."

Juana Inés walked like a somnambulist toward Padre Antonio, her victory over the professors dragging behind her, heavy as a cross.

"Please forgive me, my dear," the Viceroy said. "I had no idea the tournament would result in this. I trust that Padre Antonio," and at this the Viceroy cast a sidelong sneer at the priest, "will not condemn my soul if I congratulate you for a performance that not only exceeded my wildest expectations but also increased my admiration for your talents, and, I'm sure, won you the respect of your colleagues; for, despite your sex and your age, you are, indeed, their colleague, my dear."

From the courtyard came the keening of the guitars. The Viceroy lifted her hand to his lips and brushed his mustache over her fingers. When he had gone, Padre Antonio raised his right hand over Juana Inés's face. She flinched, expecting the priest to strike her, but he only drew a cross in midair, her doom or her salvation.

"I know you are no heretic, Child. And I understand the Viceroy's point about your memory and your voracious appetite for books. I have, therefore, a proposition to make, a way of directing your mind toward higher learning while saving your soul at the same time. How would you like to be a bride?"

"Marriage?" screeched Juana Inés.

"The ultimate marriage," said the priest, his eyes glittering like flints of obsidian.

She closed her eyes and imagined a man's hands on her body. A man's lips and beard on her face. Her belly swelling with children. Her mind shriveling like a prune. "Oh, no, Father!" she cried, clutching at his wide sleeves, "please, don't make me get married. I'd rather burn at the stake like Joan of Arc. Please, Father."

"An earthly marriage is not what I mean. In that black dress, I see a humble and obedient bride of Christ, of the Carmelite order, perhaps. *Yes*, the Carmelites will cleanse that vanity of yours that has led you into dangerous waters."

"Carmelites, Father?" Juana Inés felt her lungs contract in her rib cage.

Padre Antonio looked up at the candles in the chandelier and made the triple sign of the cross. "I see, now, the infinite wisdom of your plan, O Lord," Padre Antonio seemed to chant.

"But I'm registered as a daughter of the church, Padre," said Juana Inés. "I have no father, no dowry; I could never be a nun. I'm . . ." What was she? . . . What else could she be? . . . "I'm a sinner, Padre."

"Of course you are, my daughter," said Padre Antonio, "of course you are."

FROM THE
VEINS OF
LOS ABUELOS

She has always said to me, "Remember your dreams because they have special meaning. Remember the yerbas that grow in the wild, how they work, when to use them. . . ."

—Rosa Elena Yzquierdo, "Abuela"

ABUELA

Rosa Elena Yzquierdo

Rosa Elena Yzquierdo is author of poems and short stories, which have appeared in The Americas Review, *among other publications. "Abuela" captures the figure of the traditional grandmother as she is often depicted in Chicana/o literature: as a source of knowledge and history. Though many of us buy our tortillas in the supermarket, we still remember our abuela's hands making those "slap clap slap" sounds. As children we watched our abuelas lovingly press small round dough balls into the tortillas we later ate hot off the comal. These tortilla-making sessions often took on a significance beyond that of food preparation. I remember in my own grandmother's kitchen, it was an opportunity for me to ask her my questions within the safety of that warm room. "Abuela" portrays these moments, when the conversation carries resonance far beyond the kitchen.*

MY ABUELA BEGINS HER DAILY RITUAL WITH "SANTA MARÍA, madre de Dios . . . ." She goes outside and waters the trailing plants surrounding the rickety old fence. Yerbas are growing profusely in Folger's coffee cans and an old Motorola. Abuela comes back inside and mixes flour, salt, and shortening to make tortillas for me. One of the tortillas cooking on the comal fills with air.

"That means you're going to get married," she says, then continues to knead and cook each tortilla with care, making sure to bless the first one of the stack.

"Abuela, I had a dream about fleas. What does it mean?"

"It means you're going to get some money, mija."

"Abuela, my stomach hurts."

"Te doy un tesito mija?"

She picks the yerbas, prepares them, and makes a tea for me. No smell to it, but it tastes of milk of magnesia—maybe worse.

"Drink this tea every morning for nine days before breakfast, and your stomach-aches will disappear for one year."

She has always said to me, "Remember your dreams because they have special meaning. Remember the yerbas that grow in the wild, how they work, when to use them. Remember the cures for evil eye, fright, and fever.

"Sweep the herbs across the body and repeat three Apostle's Creeds to drive out evil spirits. Crack an egg in a glass of water and say three Hail Marys to take away evil eye and fever. Remember these things. They are all a part of you—a part of your heritage."

She said once, "Yo soy mexicana; tu mamá es mexicana pero tú eres americana."

I just try to hold on.

"Understand, understand, don't be like the Americanos, they have to understand everything. It was a lesson, a miracle or a mystery. Just believe in mysteries, and you'll live a long time." . . .

—Orlando Romero, "Nubes," from *Nambé—Year One*

NUBES

from *NAMBÉ—YEAR ONE*

Orlando Romero

Orlando Romero *is a columnist for the* Santa Fe Reporter *and director of the History Library in the Place of the Governors in Santa Fe. He has been an* NEA *fellow in creative writing (1977) and a fellow in the New Mexico Eminent Scholars Program (1990). Author of the novel* Nambé—Year One *(1976), he is currently working on two books: a collection of short stories called* The Day of the Wind; *and a history of adobe as seen through the poet's eye.*

"Nubes," a chapter from Nambé—Year One, *portrays a young boy's relationship with his grandfather and their connection over a* descanso. *A* descanso *literally means a resting place, but is also the word for the crosses that line the roadside and indicate where individuals have died. The markers tell shepherds where to stop and rest. Romero says of this selection, " 'Nubes' is an important chapter in which I dealt with my mother's loss of my father. My father was not there for her, and she turned that absence into caring by caring even more for her children—which made me even stronger. But the most important thing was that through my grandfather's story I came to the realization that one has to have a most enormous amount of faith to get through life and that life is mysterious and exemplary; it teaches through example and one shouldn't strive to understand everything."*

IN THE PELTING RAIN I SAW MY MOTHER'S PETUNIAS MELT INTO THE
brownness of the earth. Nambé receives its life and passion from
the sun. It rains little here. When it does rain, the inhabitants
and dwellers of this ancient place take on different appearances.
The forehead of the face hangs obtrusively on the brow. The
color of living complexion turns gray like the sky and the eye
sockets turn black like the storm. The gentleness is replaced by
the heaviness of darkened spirits. It shows in their movements.
Sparks fly at the darkened skies.

Viable, reflexive, warm muscles are now trapped in cages.
Their adobe house, or womb, is warm. But they look out with
longing eyes and tired sighs; their goats, cows, horses and plows
sit unmoving. In one day's rain the soul of these inhabitants will
begin to gather rust.

I sit by the corner fireplace, watching the piñon flames
burn the air around them. My cat purrs in his dreams.
His tail switches, then his leg. He dreams of the cat next
door.

Here in Nambé, we all dream. Some of us in the middle of
the sun, some of us under black storms. My Grandfather dreams
as he nervously paces the floor. He longs for his fields.

My Mother sits on the rocking chair in the corner. She's
looking at her book pretending she is reading. In reality, she
dreams. Her smile is warm and gentle. Her eyes are lonely and
longing, and though her body is young and strong she always
looks tired. She works hard. Whenever I can, I help her clean
the rich doctor's house and the other millionaires' houses that
are scattered throughout the valley.

They say they like to live like us. Adobe houses, corner
fireplaces, vigas and all the other materials that surround us.
They, too, like our 'charm.' The essence they will never see;
the living and dying of it they will never feel. Some don't care

to. There are exceptions; the doctor's wife is gentle, kind and understanding. She reminds me of my Mother.

In dreams of gentle smiles, with piñon flames licking the foundation of memory and the warmth of our adobe womb, I dream in the longing of my Mother's thoughts.

"How am I so wrong for him? He drinks and drinks. I don't make him happy. He finds no peace here at home. I wonder how he's doing in California? Six months now, not a word. Doesn't he realize he's my only man? No one kisses my breasts, no one talks to me in the lateness of the evenings, no man makes me laugh like he does. That first year, it was so fine, so rich and gentle. What distracted him? Why can't he raise himself above it, instead of drinking himself below it?"

In her longing glances and the warmth of our fire, I wonder where my Father is. My memories of him are mixed between the good and the confused. No one takes me fishing up to the beaver ponds now, or lets me shoot the twenty-two. I wonder what California is like? Why doesn't he send me a pocketknife or a yo-yo, like he said he would?

Denying memory and the sorrow that haunts, not realities, but appearances, illusions, and what appears to be the surface of auras, I ask my Grandfather to tell me a story.

"Grandfather, tell me a story, when you were little like me, when you lived in Las Trampas with your goats."

His pacing stopped, the color of the sun returned to his face because there was nothing that brought him more joy than to remember his childhood. He walked to the old trastero he had carved. From it he took a piece of dried meat for both of us. Then with his enormous golden and calloused hands he gestured for me to move so that we could both sit on the adobe banco near the corner fireplace.

In his closeness to me, his presence was as soothing as the ancient herbal medicines he put into his words.

"Let's see, have I told you about the time we had a billy goat with four horns and what happened to me with a descanso?"

"No, what's a descanso, Grandpa?"

"You know what a descanso is. You see them on the highway all the time. A descanso is a cross marking the place where a person has died."

"You mean where he is buried, Grandpa?"

"No, no, it just marks the place where a person has died. Listen carefully to me, Mateo, I know you may forget because there have been times when I've been reckless with the things I should have remembered."

In his pause he glanced outside the window. The storm might end after his story.

"Anyway I was about your age and my Father had given me charge of forty or fifty goats. Among them we had a wild and strange billy goat. From the day he was born he was strange. His mother had never been with another male or macho before, yet she still had him, and stranger yet, as he grew older there appeared four horns on his head, instead of two. He was more than mischievous, most of the time we had to keep him locked up in the pen by himself. One day he almost broke your Great Grandfather's ribs. He butted unexpectedly and from that day on we were warned he might kill one of us with his strength and cunning. But, because those days were full of strange and mysterious things around us, we thought nothing of it. Yet, we always respected him."

Between the battle of the jerky and his old teeth, my Grandfather continued the story.

"Well, one day, I took the herd of goats with the billy goat about three miles from our home, up to a high valley plateau. Here the pasture was tall and there was a stream that cut the green valley in halves. It was like a green emerald. It was full of peace and calm with the birds and noises of Summer stinging the stillness of the air with music.

"The goats were browsing peacefully, but, like goats, we never stayed in one place very long. The billy goat was peaceful enough that day and I could always tell where he was, just by his smell. I did think it was kind of unusual that he was so calm. Everything, in reality, was much too calm. There seemed to exist a timeless flickering green sense of being totally caught in a suspended dream. I began to tire, so I took out my pocketknife and started to carve a small Santo on an old weathered cottonwood root. But my age being what it was, I glanced around for more daring adventures, maybe some carving on something unusual.

"My eyes scanned the nearby piñon trees, and the twisted roots that seemed determined to cling to life, though some of them were only embracing barren rocks. I searched the hideously wind-formed limbs of junipers that reminded me of La Llorona's arms in her desperate, longing search for children that might never have been hers. These weren't the target for my pocketknife. Instead, my restless childish eyes focused on a tall descanso. Larger than most descansos, it was sawed and carved in the old way of carving crosses, intricate forceful designs, with swirls pointing down as if the soul might still be on the spot where it began its flight, stopped to dream, and its physical house destroyed.

"Instantly I expected a delightful thrill as I uprooted the descanso; my knife could hardly wait to put its own designs on it. Instead, the peaceful, glowing emerald of the valley was ripped apart by a lightning bolt eight or ten feet away from me. The sun disappeared into what seemed to be an intensely black crack in the sky. The goats cried as if they were being slaughtered by a dull knife. I stood terrified, numb and paralyzed in the fear that swept the valley and my soul. Maybe it lasted a minute, it felt more like a hundred years. I thought I was never going to see it again, but the sun burst through the darkness and again returned the peace and green of the emerald to the valley.

"Having been reborn, I searched for my scattered goats. I searched till it was nearly dark, fearing the whipping I was going to get for having lost the herd. I knew it was useless to search in the dark, so, exhausted, I returned home.

"There in the open pen, as well as I could tell by the falling light, were all my goats. The smell of the billy goat with the four horns still lingered, yet somehow I knew he wasn't there. Besides, he was so large his silhouette always towered above the rest of the goats. My father asked me the reasons for all the commotion, the goats running at breakneck speed and the loss of the billy goat, and my tired, dirty, old man appearance.

"When I told him about the descanso, that was as far as I had to go. He took me by the arm, took the piece of leather strap that tied the gate and was about to whip my pants when my mother caught his arm in the air. 'No,' she said, 'leave him alone. You can tell, he'll never forget it for as long as he lives.'

"Next day we got up even earlier than usual. We searched every ravine, arroyo, crevice and canyon in that valley. We never found trace of the goat with the four horns. No blood, no tracks, no struggle; it just disappeared to where it came from."

"But Grandpa, where did it go? Maybe he was the devil, Grandpa? I don't understand!"

"Understand, understand, don't be like the Americanos, they have to understand everything. It was a lesson, a miracle or a mystery. Just believe in mysteries, and you'll live a long time."

At the trail of his words, the sun broke through the storm clouds of Nambé. He looked up at the remaining clouds and said, "Estas nubes, siempre me siguen pero no les vale mojarme."

I approached the porch and noticed that Grandma was vigorously chewing something. She held a small white bag in one hand. Saying *"Qué deseas tomar?"* she withdrew a large orange gumdrop from the bag and began slowly chewing it in her toothless mouth, smacking loudly as she did so. I stood below her for a moment trying to remember the word for candy. Then it came to me: *"Dulce,"* I said. . . .

—Gerald Haslam, "The Horned Toad"

THE HORNED TOAD

Gerald Haslam

Gerald Haslam was born to a mixed Anglo Hispanic family in the Bakersfield area of California's Great Central Valley. As a boy and young man he worked in agricultural fields, in packing sheds, and in the oil fields. He has published six collections of short stories—most recently That Constant Coyote *(1990), which won a Josephine Miles Award from PEN—three collections of essays, a novel, and seven nonfiction books and anthologies. "The Horned Toad" centers around the relationship between a young English-speaking boy and his Spanish-speaking grandmother. The story is particularly significant because it depicts the historical importance of changes in language and culture within the Chicana/o community.*

In describing the way this story reflects on his own childhood, Haslam says, "I tell my Chicano companeros *that I am their grandchildren. That prospect doesn't necessarily comfort them, but they understand what I'm saying. I'm the product of a 'mixed marriage' two generations ago when taboos were much higher than today. Raised by a mother who, in turn, had been raised by her Mexican grandmother, I am more openly and proudly Hispanic than my pale skin and fair hair might suggest (I am three quarters Anglo and equally pleased with that). At home, however, Spanish*

was our secret language, Catholicism our church, la familia our real
religion. I tell my children (who add Cree, French, Polish, and
German to the mix) that we are what America is becoming. 'The
Horned Toad' is fiction based on actual events. The boy is me, the
grandmother my abuelita as I remember her. Not all the events in
the story actually happened, however; they have been shaped to
make a point: the centrality of family. It is a truth I learned at my
mother's breast and have never forgotten, for it perpetuates wisdom
lugged north in the 1850s when my great-great-grandparents
migrated from Mexico.''

"*EXPECTORAN SU SANGRE!*" EXCLAIMED GREAT-GRANDMA WHEN I
showed her the small horned toad I had removed from my
breast pocket. I turned toward my mother, who translated:
"They spit blood."

"*De los ojos,*" Grandma added. "From their eyes," Mother
explained, herself uncomfortable in the presence of the small
beast.

I grinned, "Awwwwww."

But my great-grandmother did not smile. "*Son muy toxicos,*"
she nodded with finality. Mother moved back an involuntary
step, her hands suddenly busy at her breast. "Put that thing
down," she ordered.

"His name's John," I said.

"Put John down and not in your pocket, either," my mother
nearly shouted. "Those things are very poisonous. Didn't you
understand what Grandma said?"

I shook my head.

"Well . . ." Mother looked from one of us to the other—
spanning four generations of California, standing three feet
apart—and said, "Of course you didn't. Please take him back
where you got him, and be careful. We'll all feel better when

you do." The tone of her voice told me that the discussion had ended, so I released the little reptile where I'd captured him.

During those years in Oildale, the mid-1940s, I needed only to walk across the street to find a patch of virgin desert. Neighborhood kids called it simply "the vacant lot," less than an acre without houses or sidewalks. Not that we were desperate for desert then, since we could walk into its scorched skin a mere half-mile west, north, and east. To the south, incongruously, flowed the icy Kern River, fresh from the Sierras and surrounded by riparian forest.

Ours was rich soil formed by that same Kern River as it ground Sierra granite and turned it into coarse sand, then carried it down into the valley and deposited it over millenia along its many changes of channels. The ants that built miniature volcanoes on the vacant lot left piles of tiny stones with telltale markings of black on white. Deeper than ants could dig were pools of petroleum that led to many fortunes and lured men like my father from Texas. The dry hills to the east and north sprouted forests of wooden derricks.

Despite the abundance of open land, plus the constant lure of the river where desolation and verdancy met, most kids relied on the vacant lot as their primary playground. Even with its bullheads and stinging insects, we played everything from football to kick-the-can on it. The lot actually resembled my father's head, bare in the middle but full of growth around the edges: weeds, stickers, cactuses, and a few bushes. We played our games on its sandy center, and conducted such sports as ant fights and lizard hunts on its brushy periphery.

That spring, when I discovered the lone horned toad near the back of the lot, had been rough on my family. Earlier, there had been quiet, unpleasant tension between Mom and Daddy. He was a silent man, little given to emotional displays. It was difficult for him to show affection and I guess the openness of Mom's family made him uneasy. Daddy had no kin in California and rarely mentioned any in Texas. He couldn't seem to understand my mother's large, intimate family, their constant noisy concern for one another, and I think he was a little jealous of the time she gave everyone, maybe even me.

I heard her talking on the phone to my various aunts and uncles, usually in Spanish. Even though I couldn't understand—Daddy had warned her not to teach me that foreign tongue because it would hurt me in school, and she'd complied—I could sense the stress. I had been afraid they were going to divorce, since she only used Spanish to hide things from me. I'd confronted her with my suspicion, but she comforted me, saying, no, that was not the problem. They were merely deciding when it would be our turn to care for Grandma. I didn't really understand, although I was relieved.

I later learned that my great-grandmother—whom we simply called "Grandma"—had been moving from house to house within the family, trying to find a place she'd accept. She hated the city, and most of the aunts and uncles lived in Los Angeles. Our house in Oildale was much closer to the open country where she'd dwelled all her life. She had wanted to come to our place right away because she had raised my mother from a baby when my own grandmother died. But the old lady seemed unimpressed with Daddy, whom she called *"ese gringo."*

In truth, we had more room, and my dad made more money in the oil patch than almost anyone else in the family. Since my mother was the closest to Grandma, our place was the logical one for her, but Ese Gringo didn't see it that way, I guess, at least not at first. Finally, after much debate, he relented.

In any case, one windy afternoon, my Uncle Manuel and Aunt Toni drove up and deposited four-and-a-half feet of be-wigged, bejeweled Spanish spitfire: a square, pale face topped by a tightly-curled black wig that hid a bald head—her hair having been lost to typhoid nearly sixty years before—her small white hands veined with rivers of blue. She walked with a prancing bounce that made her appear half her age, and she barked orders in Spanish from the moment she emerged from Manuel and Toni's car. Later, just before they left, I heard Uncle Manuel tell my dad, "Good luck, Charlie. That old lady's dynamite." Daddy only grunted.

She had been with us only two days when I tried to impress her with my horned toad. In fact, nothing I did seemed to impress her, and she referred to me as *el malcriado*, causing my mother to shake her head. Mom explained to me that Grandma was just old and lonely for Grandpa and uncomfortable in town. Mom told me that Grandma had lived over half a century in the country, away from the noise, away from clutter, away from people. She refused to accompany my mother on shopping trips, or anywhere else. She even refused to climb into a car, and I wondered how Uncle Manuel had managed to load her up in order to bring her to us.

She disliked sidewalks and roads, dancing across them when she had to, then appearing to wipe her feet on earth or grass. Things too civilized simply did not please her. A brother of hers had been killed in the great San Francisco earthquake and that had been the end of her tolerance of cities. Until my great-grandfather died, they lived on a small rancho near Arroyo Cantua, north of Coalinga. Grandpa, who had come north from Sonora as a youth to work as a *vaquero*, had bred horses and cattle, and cowboyed for other ranchers, scraping together enough of a living to raise eleven children.

He had been, until the time of his death, a lean, dark-skinned man with wide shoulders, a large nose, and a sweeping handle-bar mustache that was white when I knew him. His Indian blood darkened all his progeny so that not even I was as fair-skinned as my great-grandmother, Ese Gringo for a father or not.

As it turned out, I didn't really understand very much about Grandma at all. She was old, of course, yet in many ways my parents treated her as though she were younger than me, walking her to the bathroom at night and bringing her presents from the store. In other ways—drinking wine at dinner, for example—she was granted adult privileges. Even Daddy didn't drink wine except on special occasions. After Grandma moved in, though, he began to occasionally join her for a glass, sometimes even sitting with her on the porch for a premeal sip.

She held court on our front porch, often gazing toward the desert hills east of us or across the street at kids playing on the lot. Occasionally, she would rise, cross the yard and sidewalk and street, skip over them, sometimes stumbling on the curb, and wipe her feet on the lot's sandy soil, then she would slowly circle the boundary between the open middle and the brushy sides, searching for something, it appeared. I never figured out what.

One afternoon I returned from school and saw Grandma perched on the porch as usual, so I started to walk around the house to avoid her sharp, mostly incomprehensible, tongue. She had already spotted me. *"Venga aqui!"* she ordered, and I understood.

I approached the porch and noticed that Grandma was vigorously chewing something. She held a small white bag in one hand. Saying *"Qué deseas tomar?"* she withdrew a large orange gumdrop from the bag and began slowly chewing it in her toothless mouth, smacking loudly as she did so. I stood below her for a moment trying to remember the word for candy. Then it came to me: *"Dulce,"* I said.

Still chewing, Grandma replied, *"Mande?"*

Knowing she wanted a complete sentence, I again struggled, then came up with *"Deseo dulce."*

She measured me for a moment, before answering in nearly perfect English, "Oh, so you wan' some candy. Go to the store an' buy some."

I don't know if it was the shock of hearing her speak English for the first time, or the way she had denied me a piece of candy, but I suddenly felt tears warm my cheeks and I sprinted into the house and found Mom, who stood at the kitchen sink. "Grandma just talked English," I burst between light sobs.

"What's wrong?" she asked as she reached out to stroke my head.

"Grandma can talk English," I repeated.

"Of course she can," Mom answered. "What's wrong?"

I wasn't sure what was wrong, but after considering, I told Mom that Grandma had teased me. No sooner had I said that than the old woman appeared at the door and hiked her skirt. Attached to one of her petticoats by safety pins were several small tobacco sacks, the white cloth kind that closed with yellow drawstrings. She carefully unhooked one and opened it, withdrawing a dollar, then handed the money to me. *"Para su dulce,"* she said. Then, to my mother, she asked, "Why does he bawl like a motherless calf?"

"It's nothing," Mother replied.

"Do not weep, little one," the old lady comforted me, "Jesus and the Virgin love you." She smiled and patted my head. To my mother she said as though just realizing it, "Your baby?"

Somehow that day changed everything. I wasn't afraid of my great-grandmother any longer and, once I began spending time with her on the porch, I realized that my father had also begun directing increased attention to the old woman. Almost every evening Ese Gringo was sharing wine with Grandma. They talked out there, but I never did hear a real two-way conversation between them. Usually Grandma rattled on and Daddy nodded. She'd chuckle and pat his hand and he might grin, even grunt a word or two, before she'd begin talking again. Once I saw my mother standing by the front window watching them together, a smile playing across her face.

No more did I sneak around the house to avoid Grandma after school. Instead, she waited for me and discussed my efforts in class gravely, telling Mother that I was a bright boy, *"muy inteligente,"* and that I should be sent to the nuns who would train me. I would make a fine priest. When Ese Gringo heard that, he smiled and said, "He'd make a fair-to-middlin' Holy Roller preacher, too." Even Mom had to chuckle, and my great-grandmother shook her finger at Ese Gringo. "Oh you debil, Sharlie!" she cackled.

Frequently, I would accompany Grandma to the lot where she would explain that no fodder could grow there. Poor pasture or not, the lot was at least unpaved, and Grandma greeted even the tiniest new cactus or flowering weed with joy. "Look how beautiful," she would croon. "In all this ugliness, it lives." Oildale was my home and it didn't look especially ugly to me, so I could only grin and wonder.

Because she liked the lot and things that grew there, I showed her the horned toad when I captured it a second time. I was determined to keep it, although I did not discuss my plans with anyone. I also wanted to hear more about the bloody eyes, so I thrust the small animal nearly into her face one afternoon. She did not flinch. *"Ola señor sangre de ojos,"* she said with a mischievous grin. *"Qué tal?"* It took me a moment to catch on.

"You were kidding before," I accused.

"Of course," she acknowledged, still grinning.

"But why?"

"Because the little beast belongs with his own kind in his own place, not in your pocket. Give him his freedom, my son."

I had other plans for the horned toad, but I was clever enough not to cross Grandma. "Yes, Ma'am," I replied. That night I placed the reptile in a flower bed cornered by a brick wall Ese Gringo had built the previous summer. It was a spot rich with insects for the toad to eat, and the little wall, only a foot high, must have seemed massive to so squat an animal.

Nonetheless, the next morning, when I searched for the horned toad it was gone. I had no time to explore the yard for it, so I trudged off to school, my belly troubled. How could it have escaped? Classes meant little to me that day. I thought only of my lost pet—I had changed his name to Juan, the same as my great-grandfather—and where I might find him.

I shortened my conversation with Grandma that afternoon so I could search for Juan. "What do you seek?" the old woman asked me as I poked through flower beds beneath the porch. "Praying mantises," I improvised, and she merely nodded, surveying me. But I had eyes only for my lost pet, and I continued pushing through branches and brushing aside leaves. No luck.

Finally, I gave in and turned toward the lot. I found my horned toad nearly across the street, crushed. It had been heading for the miniature desert and had almost made it when an automobile's tire had run over it. One notion immediately swept me: if I had left it on its lot, it would still be alive. I stood rooted there in the street, tears slicking my cheeks, and a car honked its horn as it passed, the driver shouting at me.

Grandma joined me, and stroked my back. "The poor little beast," was all she said, then she bent slowly and scooped up what remained of the horned toad and led me out of the street. "We must return him to his own place," she explained, and we trooped, my eyes still clouded, toward the back of the vacant lot. Carefully, I dug a hole with a piece of wood. Grandma placed Juan in it and covered him. We said an Our Father and a Hail Mary, then Grandma walked me back to the house. "Your little Juan is safe with God, my son," she comforted. We kept the horned toad's death a secret, and we visited his small grave frequently.

Grandma fell just before school ended and summer vacation began. As was her habit, she had walked alone to the vacant lot but this time, on her way back, she tripped over the curb and broke her hip. That following week, when Daddy brought her home from the hospital, she seemed to have shrunken. She sat hunched in a wheelchair on the porch, gazing with faded eyes toward the hills or at the lot, speaking rarely. She still sipped wine every evening with Daddy and even I could tell how concerned he was about her. It got to where he'd look in on her before leaving for work every morning and again at night before turning in. And if Daddy was home, Grandma always wanted him to push her chair when she needed moving, calling, "Sharlie!" until he arrived.

I was tugged from sleep on the night she died by voices drumming through the walls into darkness. I couldn't understand them, but was immediately frightened by the uncommon sounds of words in the night. I struggled from bed and walked into the living room just as Daddy closed the front door and a car pulled away.

Mom was sobbing softly on the couch and Daddy walked to her, stroked her head, then noticed me. "Come here, son," he gently ordered.

I walked to him and, uncharacteristically, he put an arm around me. "What's wrong?" I asked, near tears myself. Mom looked up, but before she could speak, Daddy said, "Grandma died." Then he sighed heavily and stood there with his arms around his weeping wife and son.

The next day my Uncle Manuel and Uncle Arnulfo, plus Aunt Chintia, arrived and over food they discussed with my mother where Grandma should be interred. They argued that it would be too expensive to transport her body home and, besides, they could more easily visit her grave if she was buried in Bakersfield. "They have such a nice, manicured grounds at Greenlawn," Aunt Chintia pointed out. Just when it seemed they had agreed, I could remain silent no longer. "But Grandma has to go home," I burst. "She has to! It's the only thing she really wanted. We can't leave her in the city."

Uncle Arnulfo, who was on the edge, snapped to Mother that I belonged with the other children, not interrupting adult conversation. Mom quietly agreed, but I refused. My father walked into the room then. "What's wrong?" he asked.

"They're going to bury Grandma in Bakersfield, Daddy. Don't let 'em, please."

"Well, son . . ."

"When my horny toad got killed and she helped me to bury it, she said we had to return him to his place."

"Your horny toad?" Mother asked.

"He got squished and me and Grandma buried him in the lot. She said we had to take him back to his place. Honest she did."

No one spoke for a moment, then my father, Ese Gringo, who stood against the sink, responded: "That's right . . ." he paused, then added, "We'll bury her." I saw a weary smile cross my mother's face. "If she wanted to go back to the ranch then that's where we have to take her," Daddy said.

I hugged him and he, right in front of everyone, hugged back.

No one argued. It seemed, suddenly, as though they had all wanted to do exactly what I had begged for. Grown-ups baffled me. Late that week the entire family, hundreds it seemed, gathered at the little Catholic church in Coalinga for mass, then drove out to Arroyo Cantua and buried Grandma next to Grandpa. She rests there today.

My mother, father, and I drove back to Oildale that afternoon across the scorching westside desert, through sand and tumbleweeds and heat shivers. Quiet and sad, we knew we had done our best. Mom, who usually sat next to the door in the front seat, snuggled close to Daddy, and I heard her whisper to him, "Thank you, Charlie," as she kissed his cheek.

Daddy squeezed her, hesitated as if to clear his throat, then answered, "When you're family, you take care of your own."

But this was a different kind of help, Amá said, because Abuelita was dying. Looking into her gray eye, then into her brown one, the doctor said it was just a matter of days. And so it seemed only fair that these hands she had melted and formed found use in rubbing her caving body. . . .

—Helena Maria Viramontes, "The Moths"

THE MOTHS

Helena Maria Viramontes

Helena Maria Viramontes *has been coordinator of the Los Angeles Latino Writers Association, literary editor of* XismeArte Magazine, *and winner of several literary awards, including the University of California, Irvine Chicano Literary Contest. She is coeditor of* Chicana Creativity and Criticism: Charting New Frontiers in American Literature *(1988). "The Moths" is taken from* The Moths and Other Stories *(1985). In Mexican culture, death is not to be feared. Consequently, death is a favorite subject of Chicana/o literature. Dia de los muertos/Day of the Dead is a holiday in which there are two days of festivities and celebrations. Elaborate altars are made, some with pictures of the family members or friends who have died, along with objects associated with the deceased, such as favorite foods and toys.*

Viramontes says of the influence of her childhood on her writing: "Depending on the circumstances, my role as a writer is like a chameleon. Coming from a family of eleven, my father was very strict with us. To keep us in check (we were a female majority), he had a quarter-inch-thick correa in which he carved handles with a single-edged razor blade. It sat above his beloved tape recorder on the bed stand. If one of us got in trouble, we were all lined up and punished for that one infraction with a swift, hurtful nalgaso. This is not to say that this element of discipline is recommended, but given who I am, I would venture to say that this developed a certain amount of collective responsibility among us. We were made to watch out for one another in a way that made us responsible for each other's behavior, because in my father's eyes, we were. These elements of collective responsibility spilled over to the community at large."

I WAS FOURTEEN YEARS OLD WHEN ABUELITA REQUESTED MY HELP. And it seemed only fair. Abuelita had pulled me through the rages of scarlet fever by placing, removing and replacing potato slices on the temples of my forehead; she had seen me through several whippings, an arm broken by a dare jump off Tío Enrique's toolshed, puberty, and my first lie. Really, I told Amá, it was only fair.

Not that I was her favorite granddaughter or anything special. I wasn't even pretty or nice like my older sisters and I just couldn't do the girl things they could do. My hands were too big to handle the fineries of crocheting or embroidery and I always pricked my fingers or knotted my colored threads time and time again while my sisters laughed and called me bull hands with their cute waterlike voices. So I began keeping a piece of jagged brick in my sock to bash my sisters or anyone who called me bull hands. Once, while we all sat in the bedroom, I hit Teresa on the forehead, right above her eyebrow and she ran to Amá with her mouth open, her hand over her eye while blood seeped between her fingers. I was used to the whippings by then.

I wasn't respectful either. I even went so far as to doubt the power of Abuelita's slices, the slices she said absorbed my fever. "You're still alive, aren't you?" Abuelita snapped back, her pasty gray eye beaming at me and burning holes in my suspicions. Regretful that I had let secret questions drop out of my mouth, I couldn't look into her eyes. My hands began to fan out, grow like a liar's nose until they hung by my side like low weights. Abuelita made a balm out of dried moth wings and Vicks and rubbed my hands, shaped them back to size and it was the strangest feeling. Like bones melting. Like sun shining through the darkness of your eyelids. I didn't mind helping Abuelita after that, so Amá would always send me over to her.

In the early afternoon Amá would push her hair back, hand me my sweater and shoes, and tell me to go to Mama Luna's. This was to avoid another fight and another whipping, I knew. I would deliver one last shot on Marisela's arm and jump out of our house, the slam of the screen door burying her cries of anger, and I'd gladly go help Abuelita plant her wild lilies or jasmine or heliotrope or cilantro or hierbabuena in red Hills Brothers coffee cans. Abuelita would wait for me at the top step of her porch holding a hammer and nail and empty coffee cans. And although we hardly spoke, hardly looked at each other as we worked over root transplants, I always felt her gray eye on me. It made me feel, in a strange sort of way, safe and guarded and not alone. Like God was supposed to make you feel.

On Abuelita's porch, I would puncture holes in the bottom of the coffee cans with a nail and a precise hit of a hammer. This completed, my job was to fill them with red clay mud from beneath her rose bushes, packing it softly, then making a perfect hole, four fingers round, to nest a sprouting avocado pit, or the spidery sweet potatoes that Abuelita rooted in mayonnaise jars with toothpicks and daily water, or prickly chayotes that produced vines that twisted and wound all over her porch pillars, crawling to the roof, up and over the roof, and down the other side, making her small brick house look like it was cradled within the vines that grew pear-shaped squashes ready for the pick, ready to be steamed with onions and cheese and butter. The roots would burst out of the rusted coffee cans and search for a place to connect. I would then feed the seedlings with water.

But this was a different kind of help, Amá said, because Abuelita was dying. Looking into her gray eye, then into her brown one, the doctor said it was just a matter of days. And so it seemed only fair that these hands she had melted and formed found use in rubbing her caving body with alcohol and marihuana, rubbing her arms and legs, turning her face to the window so that she could watch the Bird of Paradise blooming or smell the scent of clove in the air. I toweled her face frequently and held her hand for hours. Her gray wiry hair hung over the mattress. Since I could remember, she'd kept her long hair in braids. Her mouth was vacant and when she slept, her eyelids never closed all the way. Up close, you could see her gray eye beaming out the window, staring hard as if to remember everything. I never kissed her. I left the window open when I went to the market.

Across the street from Jay's Market there was a chapel. I never knew its denomination, but I went in just the same to search for candles. I sat down on one of the pews because there were none. After I cleaned my fingernails, I looked up at the high ceiling. I had forgotten the vastness of these places, the coolness of the marble pillars and the frozen statues with blank eyes. I was alone. I knew why I had never returned.

That was one of Apá's biggest complaints. He would pound his hands on the table, rocking the sugar dish or spilling a cup of coffee and scream that if I didn't go to mass every Sunday to save my goddamn sinning soul, then I had no reason to go out of the house, period. Punto final. He would grab my arm and dig his nails into me to make sure I understood the importance of catechism. Did he make himself clear? Then he strategically directed his anger at Amá for her lousy ways of bringing up daughters, being disrespectful and unbelieving, and my older sisters would pull me aside and tell me if I didn't get to mass right this minute, they were all going to kick the holy shit out of me. Why am I so selfish? Can't you see what it's doing to Amá, you idiot? So I would wash my feet and stuff them in my black Easter shoes that shone with Vaseline, grab a missal and veil, and wave good-bye to Amá.

I would walk slowly down Lorena to First to Evergreen, counting the cracks on the cement. On Evergreen I would turn left and walk to Abuelita's. I liked her porch because it was shielded by the vines of the chayotes and I could get a good look at the people and car traffic on Evergreen without them knowing. I would jump up the porch steps, knock on the screen door as I wiped my feet and call Abuelita? mi Abuelita? As I opened the door and stuck my head in, I would catch the gagging scent of toasting chile on the placa. When I entered the sala, she would greet me from the kitchen, wringing her hands in her apron. I'd sit at the corner of the table to keep from being in her way. The chiles made my eyes water. Am I crying? No, Mama Luna, I'm sure not crying. I don't like going to mass, but my eyes watered anyway, the tears dropping on the tablecloth like candle wax. Abuelita lifted the burnt chiles from the fire and sprinkled water on them until the skins began to separate. Placing them in front of me, she turned to check the menudo. I peeled the skins off and put the flimsy, limp-looking green and yellow chiles in the molcajete and began to crush and crush and twist and crush the heart out of the tomato, the clove of garlic, the stupid chiles that made me cry, crushed them until they turned into liquid under my bull hand. With a wooden spoon, I scraped hard to destroy the guilt, and my tears were gone. I put the bowl of chile next to a vase filled with freshly cut roses. Abuelita touched my hand and pointed to the bowl of menudo that steamed in front of me. I spooned some chile into the menudo and rolled a corn tortilla thin with the palms of my hands. As I ate, a fine Sunday breeze entered the kitchen and a rose petal calmly feathered down to the table.

I left the chapel without blessing myself and walked to Jay's. Most of the time Jay didn't have much of anything. The tomatoes were always soft and the cans of Campbell soups had rusted spots on them. There was dust on the tops of cereal boxes. I picked up what I needed: rubbing alcohol, five cans of chicken broth, a big bottle of Pine Sol. At first Jay got mad because I thought I had forgotten the money. But it was there all the time, in my back pocket.

When I returned from the market, I heard Amá crying in Abuelita's kitchen. She looked up at me with puffy eyes. I placed the bags of groceries on the table and began putting the cans of soup away. Amá sobbed quietly. I never kissed her. After a while, I patted her on the back for comfort. Finally: "¿Y mi Amá?" she asked in a whisper, then choked again and cried into her apron.

Abuelita fell off the bed twice yesterday, I said, knowing that I shouldn't have said it and wondering why I wanted to say it because it only made Amá cry harder. I guess I became angry and just so tired of the quarrels and beatings and unanswered prayers and my hands just there hanging helplessly by my side. Amá looked at me again, confused, angry, and her eyes were filled with sorrow. I went outside and sat on the porch swing and watched the people pass. I sat there until she left. I dozed off repeating the words to myself like rosary prayers: when do you stop giving when do you start giving when do you . . . and when my hands fell from my lap, I awoke to catch them. The sun was setting, an orange glow, and I knew Abuelita was hungry.

There comes a time when the sun is defiant. Just about the time when moods change, inevitable seasons of a day, transitions from one color to another, that hour or minute or second when the sun is finally defeated, finally sinks into the realization that it cannot with all its power to heal or burn, exist forever, there comes an illumination where the sun and earth meet, a final burst of burning red orange fury reminding us that although endings are inevitable, they are necessary for rebirths, and when that time came, just when I switched on the light in the kitchen to open Abuelita's can of soup, it was probably then that she died.

The room smelled of Pine Sol and vomit and Abuelita had defecated the remains of her cancerous stomach. She had turned to the window and tried to speak, but her mouth remained open and speechless. I heard you, Abuelita, I said, stroking her cheek, I heard you. I opened the windows of the house and let the soup simmer and overboil on the stove. I turned the stove off and poured the soup down the sink. From the cabinet I got a tin basin, filled it with lukewarm water and carried it carefully to the room. I went to the linen closet and took out some modest bleached white towels. With the sacredness of a priest preparing his vestments, I unfolded the towels one by one on my shoulders. I removed the sheets and blankets from her bed and peeled off her thick flannel nightgown. I toweled her puzzled face, stretching out the wrinkles, removing the coils of her neck, toweled her shoulders and breasts. Then I changed the water. I returned to towel the creases of her stretch-marked stomach, her sporadic vaginal hairs, and her sagging thighs. I removed the lint from between her toes and noticed a mapped birthmark on the fold of her buttock. The scars on her back which were as thin as the life lines on the palms of her hands made me realize how little I really knew of Abuelita. I covered her with a thin blanket and went into the bathroom. I washed my hands, and turned on the tub faucets and watched the water pour into the tub with vitality and steam. When it was full, I turned off the water and undressed. Then, I went to get Abuelita.

She was not as heavy as I thought and when I carried her in my arms, her body fell into a V, and yet my legs were tired, shaky, and I felt as if the distance between the bedroom and bathroom was miles and years away. Amá, where are you?

I stepped into the bathtub one leg first, then the other. I bent my knees slowly to descend into the water slowly so I wouldn't scald her skin. There, there, Abuelita, I said, cradling her, smoothing her as we descended, I heard you. Her hair fell back and spread across the water like eagle's wings. The water in the tub overflowed and poured onto the tile of the floor. Then the moths came. Small, gray ones that came from her soul and out through her mouth fluttering to light, circling the single dull light bulb of the bathroom. Dying is lonely and I wanted to go to where the moths were, stay with her and plant chayotes whose vines would crawl up her fingers and into the clouds; I wanted to rest my head on her chest with her stroking my hair, telling me about the moths that lay within the soul and slowly eat the spirit up; I wanted to return to the waters of the womb with her so that we would never be alone again. I wanted. I wanted my Amá. I removed a few strands of hair from Abuelita's face and held her small light head within the hollow of my neck. The bathroom was filled with moths, and for the first time in a long time I cried, rocking us, crying for her, for me, for Amá, the sobs emerging from the depths of anguish, the misery of feeling half born, sobbing until finally the sobs rippled into circles and circles of sadness and relief. There, there, I said to Abuelita, rocking us gently, there, there.

"Where's Grandpa?" I asked Grandma, looking down at the floor so she wouldn't ask me why I'd been crying. She was sewing on a quilt and didn't look up.

"I think he's out back working in the bean field."

I went outside and looked out at the fields. There he was. I could see him walking between the rows, his body bent over the little plants, hoe in hand. I walked slowly out to him, trying to think how I could best ask him for the money. . . .

—Marta Salinas, "The Scholarship Jacket"

THE SCHOLARSHIP JACKET

Marta Salinas

Marta Salinas's stories have appeared in the Los Angeles Herald Examiner *and in* California Living. *Historically, bilingual students have been punished for speaking Spanish, and often have not been given the opportunities afforded to those whose native language is English. The difficulties of transcending the stereotypes, as well as the real economic limitations, of one's class are also described in this story of a young girl's struggle for recognition.*

THE SMALL TEXAS SCHOOL THAT I ATTENDED CARRIED OUT A tradition every year during the eighth grade graduation; a beautiful gold and green jacket, the school colors, was awarded to the class valedictorian, the student who had maintained the highest grades for eight years. The scholarship jacket had a big gold S on the left front side and the winner's name was written in gold letters on the pocket.

My oldest sister Rosie had won the jacket a few years back and I fully expected to win also. I was fourteen and in the eighth grade. I had been a straight A student since the first grade, and the last year I had looked forward to owning that jacket. My father was a farm laborer who couldn't earn enough money to feed eight children, so when I was six I was given to my grandparents to raise. We couldn't participate in sports at school because there were registration fees, uniform costs, and trips out of town; so even though we were quite agile and athletic, there would never be a sports school jacket for us. This one, the scholarship jacket, was our only chance.

In May, close to graduation, spring fever struck, and no one paid any attention in class; instead we stared out the windows and at each other, wanting to speed up the last few weeks of school. I despaired every time I looked in the mirror. Pencil thin, not a curve anywhere, I was called "Beanpole" and "String Bean" and I knew that's what I looked like. A flat chest, no hips, and a brain, that's what I had. That really isn't much for a fourteen-year-old to work with, I thought, as I absentmindedly wandered from my history class to the gym. Another hour of sweating in basketball and displaying my toothpick legs was coming up. Then I remembered my P.E. shorts were still in a bag under my desk where I'd forgotten them. I had to walk all the way back and get them. Coach Thompson was a real bear if anyone wasn't dressed for P.E. She had said I was a good forward and once she even tried to talk Grandma into letting me join the team. Grandma, of course, said no.

I was almost back at my classroom's door when I heard angry voices and arguing. I stopped. I didn't mean to eavesdrop; I just hesitated, not knowing what to do. I needed those shorts and I was going to be late, but I didn't want to interrupt an argument between my teachers. I recognized the voices: Mr. Schmidt, my history teacher, and Mr. Boone, my math teacher. They seemed to be arguing about me. I couldn't believe it. I still remember the shock that rooted me flat against the wall as if I were trying to blend in with the graffiti written there.

"I refuse to do it! I don't care who her father is, her grades don't even begin to compare to Martha's. I won't lie or falsify records. Martha has a straight A plus average and you know it." That was Mr. Schmidt and he sounded very angry. Mr. Boone's voice sounded calm and quiet.

"Look, Joann's father is not only on the Board, he owns the only store in town; we could say it was a close tie and—"

The pounding in my ears drowned out the rest of the words, only a word here and there filtered through. ". . . Martha is Mexican. . . . resign. . . . won't do it. . . ." Mr. Schmidt came rushing out, and luckily for me went down the opposite way toward the auditorium, so he didn't see me. Shaking, I waited a few minutes and then went in and grabbed my bag and fled from the room. Mr. Boone looked up when I came in but didn't say anything. To this day I don't remember if I got in trouble in P.E. for being late or how I made it through the rest of the afternoon. I went home very sad and cried into my pillow that night so Grandmother wouldn't hear me. It seemed a cruel coincidence that I had overheard that conversation.

The next day when the principal called me into his office, I knew what it would be about. He looked uncomfortable and unhappy. I decided I wasn't going to make it any easier for him so I looked him straight in the eye. He looked away and fidgeted with the papers on his desk.

"Martha," he said, "there's been a change in policy this year regarding the scholarship jacket. As you know, it has always been free." He cleared his throat and continued. "This year the Board decided to charge fifteen dollars—which still won't cover the complete cost of the jacket."

I stared at him in shock and a small sound of dismay escaped my throat. I hadn't expected this. He still avoided looking in my eyes.

"So if you are unable to pay the fifteen dollars for the jacket, it will be given to the next one in line."

Standing with all the dignity I could muster, I said, "I'll speak to my grandfather about it, sir, and let you know tomorrow." I cried on the walk home from the bus stop. The dirt road was a quarter of a mile from the highway, so by the time I got home, my eyes were red and puffy.

"Where's Grandpa?" I asked Grandma, looking down at the floor so she wouldn't ask me why I'd been crying. She was sewing on a quilt and didn't look up.

"I think he's out back working in the bean field."

I went outside and looked out at the fields. There he was. I could see him walking between the rows, his body bent over the little plants, hoe in hand. I walked slowly out to him, trying to think how I could best ask him for the money. There was a cool breeze blowing and a sweet smell of mesquite in the air, but I didn't appreciate it. I kicked at a dirt clod. I wanted that jacket so much. It was more than just being a valedictorian and giving a little thank you speech for the jacket on graduation night. It represented eight years of hard work and expectation. I knew I had to be honest with Grandpa; it was my only chance. He saw me and looked up.

He waited for me to speak. I cleared my throat nervously and clasped my hands behind my back so he wouldn't see them shaking. "Grandpa, I have a big favor to ask you," I said in Spanish, the only language he knew. He still waited silently. I tried again. "Grandpa, this year the principal said the scholarship jacket is not going to be free. It's going to cost fifteen dollars and I have to take the money in tomorrow, otherwise it'll be given to someone else." The last words came out in an eager rush. Grandpa straightened up tiredly and leaned his chin on the hoe handle. He looked out over the field that was filled with the tiny green bean plants. I waited, desperately hoping he'd say I could have the money.

He turned to me and asked quietly, "What does a scholarship jacket mean?"

I answered quickly; maybe there was a chance. "It means you've earned it by having the highest grades for eight years and that's why they're giving it to you." Too late I realized the significance of my words. Grandpa knew that I understood it was not a matter of money. It wasn't that. He went back to hoeing the weeds that sprang up between the delicate little bean plants. It was a time consuming job; sometimes the small shoots were right next to each other. Finally he spoke again.

"Then if you pay for it, Marta, it's not a scholarship jacket, is it? Tell your principal I will not pay the fifteen dollars."

I walked back to the house and locked myself in the bathroom for a long time. I was angry with Grandfather even though I knew he was right, and I was angry with the Board, whoever they were. Why did they have to change the rules just when it was my turn to win the jacket?

It was a very sad and withdrawn girl who dragged into the principal's office the next day. This time he did look me in the eyes.

"What did your grandfather say?"

I sat very straight in my chair.

"He said to tell you he won't pay the fifteen dollars."

The principal muttered something I couldn't understand under his breath, and walked over to the window. He stood looking out at something outside. He looked bigger than usual when he stood up; he was a tall gaunt man with gray hair, and I watched the back of his head while I waited for him to speak.

"Why?" he finally asked. "Your grandfather has the money. Doesn't he own a small bean farm?"

I looked at him, forcing my eyes to stay dry. "He said if I had to pay for it, then it wouldn't be a scholarship jacket," I said and stood up to leave. "I guess you'll just have to give it to Joann." I hadn't meant to say that; it had just slipped out. I was almost to the door when he stopped me.

"Martha—wait."

I turned and looked at him, waiting. What did he want now? I could feel my heart pounding. Something bitter and vile tasting was coming up in my mouth; I was afraid I was going to be sick. I didn't need any sympathy speeches. He sighed loudly and went back to his big desk. He looked at me, biting his lip, as if thinking.

"Okay, damn it. We'll make an exception in your case. I'll tell the Board, you'll get your jacket."

I could hardly believe it. I spoke in a trembling rush. "Oh, thank you, sir!" Suddenly I felt great. I didn't know about adrenaline in those days, but I knew something was pumping through me, making me feel as tall as the sky. I wanted to yell, jump, run the mile, do something. I ran out so I could cry in the hall where there was no one to see me. At the end of the day, Mr. Schmidt winked at me and said, "I hear you're getting a scholarship jacket this year."

His face looked as happy and innocent as a baby's, but I knew better. Without answering I gave him a quick hug and ran to the bus. I cried on the walk home again, but this time because I was so happy. I couldn't wait to tell Grandpa and ran straight to the field. I joined him in the row where he was working and without saying anything I crouched down and started pulling up the weeds with my hands. Grandpa worked alongside me for a few minutes, but he didn't ask what had happened. After I had a little pile of weeds between the rows, I stood up and faced him.

"The principal said he's making an exception for me, Grandpa, and I'm getting the jacket after all. That's after I told him what you said."

Grandpa didn't say anything, he just gave me a pat on the shoulder and a smile. He pulled out the crumpled red handkerchief that he always carried in his back pocket and wiped the sweat off his forehead.

"Better go see if your grandmother needs any help with supper."

I gave him a big grin. He didn't fool me. I skipped and ran back to the house whistling some silly tune.

La Tierra
y la Escuela:
From Where
We Learn

The next morning I could hardly move. My body ached all over. I felt little control over my arms and legs. This feeling went on every morning for days until my muscles finally got used to the work.

It was Monday, the first week of November. The grape season was over and I could now go to school. I woke up early that morning and lay in bed, looking at the stars and savoring the thought of not going to work and of starting sixth grade for the first time that year. . . .

—Francisco Jiménez, "The Circuit"

THE CIRCUIT

Francisco Jiménez

F*rancisco Jiménez, an educator, teacher, administrator, and writer, has edited several anthologies, including:* The Identification and Analysis of Chicano Literature *(1979),* Hispanics in the United States: An Anthology of Creative Literature *(1979), and a collection of short stories in Spanish about life in the United States,* Mosaico de la vida: Prosa Chicana, Cubana, y Puertorriqueña *(1981). His stories have been published in journals, including* El Grito. *Jiménez is cofounder and West Coast editor of* The Bilingual Review/La Revista Bilingüe *and editorial advisor to the* Bilingual Press/Editorial Bilingüe. *In his short story "The Circuit," a child from a laboring family tries to balance work in the fields with work in the classroom. Many of our grandparents at some time had to work in the fields. Their labor shaped much of our family history as migration across state and national borders depended on the patterns of the seasons. Some families seemed to be always moving to find work. These moves affected everyone in the family, including the children.*

Jiménez says of this story: "It is a collection of recollections of my past growing up as a child in a migrant setting. Some of these were written in the form of a journal when I was an undergraduate at Santa Clara, and I wrote them because I wanted to keep in touch with my family roots. I did not want to forget that experience because it is what motivated me to work hard in acquiring my education. To be more philosophical, it was the reflection of that experience that gave meaning to my profession."

IT WAS THAT TIME OF YEAR AGAIN. ITO, THE STRAWBERRY SHARE-cropper, did not smile. It was natural. The peak of the strawberry season was over and the last few days the workers, most of them braceros, were not picking as many boxes as they had during the months of June and July.

As the last days of August disappeared, so did the number of braceros. Sunday, only one—the best picker—came to work. I liked him. Sometimes we talked during our half-hour lunch break. That is how I found out he was from Jalisco, the same state in Mexico my family was from. That Sunday was the last time I saw him.

When the sun had tired and sunk behind the mountains, Ito signaled us that it was time to go home. "Ya esora," he yelled in his broken Spanish. Those were the words I waited for twelve hours a day, every day, seven days a week, week after week. And the thought of not hearing them again saddened me.

As we drove home Papá did not say a word. With both hands on the wheel, he stared at the dirt road. My older brother, Roberto, was also silent. He leaned his head back and closed his eyes. Once in a while he cleared from his throat the dust that blew in from outside.

Yes, it was that time of year. When I opened the front door to the shack, I stopped. Everything we owned was neatly packed in cardboard boxes. Suddenly I felt even more the weight of hours, days, weeks, and months of work. I sat down on a box. The thought of having to move to Fresno and knowing what was in store for me there brought tears to my eyes.

That night I could not sleep. I lay in bed thinking about how much I hated this move.

A little before five o'clock in the morning, Papá woke everyone up. A few minutes later, the yelling and screaming of my little brothers and sisters, for whom the move was a great adventure, broke the silence of dawn. Shortly, the barking of the dogs accompanied them.

While we packed the breakfast dishes, Papá went outside to start the "Carcanchita." That was the name Papá gave his old '38 black Plymouth. He bought it in a used-car lot in Santa Rosa in the winter of 1949. Papá was very proud of his little jalopy. He had a right to be proud of it. He spent a lot of time looking at other cars before buying this one. When he finally chose the "Carcanchita," he checked it thoroughly before driving it out of the car lot. He examined every inch of the car. He listened to the motor, tilting his head from side to side like a parrot, trying to detect any noises that spelled car trouble. After being satisfied with the looks and sounds of the car, Papá then insisted on knowing who the original owner was. He never did find out from the car salesman, but he bought the car anyway. Papá figured the original owner must have been an important man because behind the rear seat of the car he found a blue necktie.

Papá parked the car out in front and left the motor running. "Listo," he yelled. Without saying a word, Roberto and I began to carry the boxes out to the car. Roberto carried the two big boxes and I carried the two smaller ones. Papá then threw the mattress on top of the car roof and tied it with ropes to the front and rear bumpers.

Everything was packed except Mamá's pot. It was an old large galvanized pot she had picked up at an army surplus store in Santa María the year I was born. The pot had many dents and nicks, and the more dents and nicks it acquired the more Mamá liked it. "Mi olla," she used to say proudly.

I held the front door open as Mamá carefully carried out her pot by both handles, making sure not to spill the cooked beans. When she got to the car, Papá reached out to help her with it. Roberto opened the rear car door and Papá gently placed it on the floor behind the front seat. All of us then climbed in. Papá sighed, wiped the sweat off his forehead with his sleeve, and said wearily: "Es todo."

As we drove away, I felt a lump in my throat. I turned around and looked at our little shack for the last time.

At sunset we drove into a labor camp near Fresno. Since Papá did not speak English, Mamá asked the camp foreman if he needed any more workers. "We don't need no more," said the foreman, scratching his head. "Check with Sullivan down the road. Can't miss him. He lives in a big white house with a fence around it."

When we got there, Mamá walked up to the house. She went through a white gate, past a row of rose bushes, up the stairs to the front door. She rang the doorbell. The porch light went on and a tall husky man came out. They exchanged a few words. After the man went in, Mamá clasped her hands and hurried back to the car. "We have work! Mr. Sullivan said we can stay there the whole season," she said, gasping and pointing to an old garage near the stables.

The garage was worn out by the years. It had no windows. The walls, eaten by termites, strained to support the roof full of holes. The dirt floor, populated by earth worms, looked like a gray road map.

That night, by the light of a kerosene lamp, we unpacked and cleaned our new home. Roberto swept away the loose dirt, leaving the hard ground. Papá plugged the holes in the walls with old newspapers and tin can tops. Mamá fed my little brothers and sisters. Papá and Roberto then brought in the mattress and placed it in the far corner of the garage. "Mamá, you and the little ones sleep on the mattress. Roberto, Panchito, and I will sleep outside under the trees," Papá said.

Early next morning Mr. Sullivan showed us where his crop was, and after breakfast, Papá, Roberto, and I headed for the vineyard to pick.

Around nine o'clock the temperature had risen to almost one hundred degrees. I was completely soaked in sweat and my mouth felt as if I had been chewing on a handkerchief. I walked over to the end of the row, picked up the jug of water we had brought, and began drinking. "Don't drink too much; you'll get sick," Roberto shouted. No sooner had he said that then I felt sick to my stomach. I dropped to my knees and let the jug roll off my hands. I remained motionless with my eyes glued on the hot sandy ground. All I could hear was the drone of insects. Slowly I began to recover. I poured water over my face and neck and watched the dirty water run down my arms to the ground.

I still felt a little dizzy when we took a break to eat lunch. It was past two o'clock and we sat underneath a large walnut tree that was on the side of the road. While we ate, Papá jotted down the number of boxes we had picked. Roberto drew designs on the ground with a stick. Suddenly I noticed Papá's face turn pale as he looked down the road. "Here comes the school bus," he whispered loudly in alarm. Instinctively, Roberto and I ran and hid in the vineyards. We did not want to get in trouble for not going to school. The neatly dressed boys about my age got off. They carried books under their arms. After they crossed the street, the bus drove away. Roberto and I came out from hiding and joined Papá. "Tienen que tener cuidado," he warned us.

After lunch we went back to work. The sun kept beating down. The buzzing insects, the wet sweat, and the hot dry dust made the afternoon seem to last forever. Finally the mountains around the valley reached out and swallowed the sun. Within an hour it was too dark to continue picking. The vines blanketed the grapes, making it difficult to see the bunches. "Vámonos," said Papá, signaling to us that it was time to quit work. Papá then took out a pencil and began to figure out how much we had earned our first day. He wrote down numbers, crossed some out, wrote down some more. "Quince," he murmured.

When we arrived home, we took a cold shower underneath a waterhose. We then sat down to eat dinner around some wooden crates that served as a table. Mamá had cooked a special meal for us. We had rice and tortillas with "carne con chile," my favorite dish.

The next morning I could hardly move. My body ached all over. I felt little control over my arms and legs. This feeling went on every morning for days until my muscles finally got used to the work.

It was Monday, the first week of November. The grape season was over and I could now go to school. I woke up early that morning and lay in bed, looking at the stars and savoring the thought of not going to work and of starting sixth grade for the first time that year. Since I could not sleep, I decided to get up and join Papá and Roberto at breakfast. I sat at the table across from Roberto, but I kept my head down. I did not want to look up and face him. I knew he was sad. He was not going to school today. He was not going tomorrow, or next week, or next month. He would not go until the cotton season was over, and that was sometime in February. I rubbed my hands together and watched the dry, acid-stained skin fall to the floor in little rolls.

When Papá and Roberto left for work, I felt relief. I walked to the top of a small grade next to the shack and watched the "Carcanchita" disappear in the distance in a cloud of dust.

Two hours later, around eight o'clock, I stood by the side of the road waiting for school bus number twenty. When it arrived I climbed in. Everyone was busy either talking or yelling. I sat in an empty seat in the back.

When the bus stopped in front of the school, I felt very nervous. I looked out the bus window and saw boys and girls carrying books under their arms. I put my hands in my pant pockets and walked to the principal's office. When I entered I heard a woman's voice say: "May I help you?" I was startled. I had not heard English for months. For a few seconds I remained speechless. I looked at the lady who waited for an answer. My first instinct was to answer her in Spanish, but I held back. Finally, after struggling for English words, I managed to tell her that I wanted to enroll in the sixth grade. After answering many questions, I was led to the classroom.

Mr. Lema, the sixth grade teacher, greeted me and assigned me a desk. He then introduced me to the class. I was so nervous and scared at that moment when everyone's eyes were on me that I wished I were with Papá and Roberto picking cotton. After taking roll, Mr. Lema gave the class the assignment for the first hour. "The first thing we have to do this morning is finish reading the story we began yesterday," he said enthusiastically. He walked up to me, handed me an English book, and asked me to read. "We are on page 125," he said politely. When I heard this, I felt my blood rush to my head; I felt dizzy. "Would you like to read?" he asked hesitantly. I opened the book to page 125. My mouth was dry. My eyes began to water. I could not begin. "You can read later," Mr. Lema said understandingly.

For the rest of the reading period I kept getting angrier and angrier with myself. I should have read, I thought to myself.

During recess I went into the restroom and opened my English book to page 125. I began to read in a low voice, pretending I was in class. There were many words I did not know. I closed the book and headed back to the classroom.

Mr. Lema was sitting at his desk correcting papers. When I entered he looked up at me and smiled. I felt better. I walked up to him and asked if he could help me with the new words. "Gladly," he said.

The rest of the month I spent my lunch hours working on English with Mr. Lema, my best friend at school.

One Friday during lunch hour Mr. Lema asked me to take a

walk with him to the music room. "Do you like music?" he asked me as we entered the building.

"Yes, I like corridos," I answered. He then picked up a trumpet, blew on it and handed it to me. The sound gave me goose bumps. I knew that sound. I had heard it in many corridos. "How would you like to learn how to play it?" he asked. He must have read my face because before I could answer, he added; "I'll teach you how to play it during our lunch hours."

That day I could hardly wait to get home to tell Papá and Mamá the great news. As I got off the bus, my little brothers and sisters ran up to meet me. They were yelling and screaming. I thought they were happy to see me, but when I opened the door to our shack, I saw that everything we owned was neatly packed in cardboard boxes.

. . . We dared not move—but when the first ant moved towards our ankles we stomped away, our Oxfords making swirls of dust that allowed us to retreat to the sidelines. But not Concha. She remained in place as big red ants crept up her shoes. One, five, ten! We stood and counted, holding our breath as the ants continued to climb. Fifteen, twenty! Twenty ants were crawling over Concha! . . .

—Mary Helen Ponce, "Concha"

CONCHA

Mary Helen Ponce

Mary Helen Ponce *has been published in journals throughout the Southwest and Mexico. Her books include a collection of short stories,* Taking Control *(1987) and* The Wedding *(1989), a novel. The author's forthcoming book is* Hoyt Street: An Autobiography *(1993). She is also working on a novel,* Raising Albuquerque. *"Concha" tells of the games in which children push themselves to their physical limits so that they can escape with harrowing stories to tell in the aftermath. Ponce says of this story: " 'Concha' was part of the original manuscript that is now* Hoyt Street. *The work is autobiographical in that Concha is a composite of two of my childhood friends that lived in Pacoima. The story speaks to the ways that we devised to have fun, growing up playing with mud, playing with ants, competing with boys to see who could best them at street games!"*

WHILE GROWING UP IN THE SMALL BARRIO OF PACOIMA MY younger brother Joey and I were left alone to find ways *para divertirnos,* to keep ourselves busy—and out of our mother's way. One way in which we whiled away long summer days was by making pea shooters. These were made from a hollow reed which we first cleaned with a piece of wire. We then collected berries from *los pirules*, the pepper trees that lined our driveway. Once we amassed enough dry berries we put them in our mouths and spat them out at each other through the pea shooter.

The berries had a terrible taste—they were even said to be poison! I was most careful not to swallow them. We selected only the hard, firm peas. The soft ones, we knew, would get mushy, crumble in our mouths and force us to gag—and lose a fight. During an important battle a short pause could spell defeat. Oftentimes while playing with Joey I watched closely. When he appeared to gag I dashed back to the pepper tree to load up on ammunition. I pelted him without mercy until he begged me to stop.

"No more. Ya no," Joey cried as he bent over to spit berries. "No more!"

"Ha, ha I got you now." I spat berries at Joey until, exhausted, we called a truce and slumped onto a wooden bench.

In fall our game came to a halt—the trees dried up; the berries fell to the ground. This was a sign for us to begin other games.

Our games were seasonal. During early spring we made whistles from the long blades of grass that grew in the open field behind our house. In winter we made dams, forts and canals from the soft mud that was our street. We tied burnt matchsticks together with string. These were our men. We positioned them along the forts (camouflaged with small branches). We also played kick the can, but our most challenging game was playing with red ants.

The ants were of the common variety: red, round and treacherous. They invaded our yard and the *llano* every summer. We always knew where ants could be found, *donde habia ormigas*. We liked to build mud and grass forts smack in the middle of ant territory. The ants were the enemy, the matchstickmen the heroes, or good guys.

Playing with ants was a real challenge! While placing our men in battle positions we timed it so as not to get bitten. We delighted in beating the ants at their own game.

Sometimes we got really brave and picked up ants with a stick, then twirled the stick around until the ants got dizzy-drunk (or so we thought)—and fell to the ground. We made ridges of dirt and pushed the ants inside, covered them with dirt and made bets as to how long it would take them to dig their way out.

Concha, my best friend and neighbor, was quite timid at school. She avoided all rough games such as kickball and Red Rover. When it came to playing with ants, however, Concha held first place for bravery. She could stand with her feet atop an anthill for the longest time! We stood trembling as ants crawled up our shoes, then quickly stomped our feet to scare them off. But Concha never lost her nerve.

One time we decided to have an ant contest. The prize was a candy bar—a Sugar Daddy sucker. We first found an anthill, lined up, then took turns standing beside the anthill while the juicy red ants climbed over our shoes. We dared not move— but when the first ant moved towards our ankles we stomped away, our Oxfords making swirls of dust that allowed us to retreat to the sidelines. But not Concha. She remained in place as big red ants crept up her shoes. One, five, ten! We stood and counted, holding our breath as the ants continued to climb. Fifteen, twenty! Twenty ants were crawling over Concha!

"*Ujule*, she sure ain't scared," cried Mundo in a hushed voice. "*No le tiene miedo a las ormigas.*"

"Uhhhhh," answered Beto, his eyes wide.

". . . I mean for a girl," added Mundo as he poked Beto in the ribs. We knew Beto liked Concha—and always came to her rescue.

We stood and counted ants. We were so caught up in this feat that we failed to notice the twenty-first ant that climbed up the back of Concha's sock . . . and bit her!

"Ay, ay, ay," screeched Concha.

"Gosh, she's gonna die," cried an alarmed Virgie as she helped stomp out ants. "She's gonna die!"

"She's too stupid to die," laughed Mundo, busy brushing ants off his feet. "She's too stupid."

"But sometimes people die when ants bite them," insisted Virgie, her face pale. "They gets real sick."

"The ants will probably die," Mundo snickered, holding his stomach and laughing loudly. "Ah, ha, ha."

"Gosh you're mean," said a shocked Virgie, hands on hips. "You are so mean."

"Yeah, but I ain't stupid."

"Come on you guys, let's get her to the *mangera*," Beto cried as he reached out to Concha who by now had decided she would live. "Come on, let's take her to the faucet."

We held Concha by the waist as she hobbled to the water faucet. Her cries were now mere whimpers as no grownup had come out to investigate. From experience we knew that if a first cry did not bring someone to our aid we should stop crying— or go home.

We helped Concha to the faucet, turned it on and began to mix water with dirt. We knew the best remedy for insect bites was *lodo*. We applied mud to all bug stings to stop the swelling. Mud was especially good for wasp stings, the yellowjackets we so feared—and from which we ran away at top speed. Whenever bees came close we stood still until they flew away, but there were no set rules on how to get rid of *avispas*. We hit out at them, and tried to scare them off but the yellowjackets were fierce! In desperation we flung dirt at them, screamed and ran home.

Not long after the ant incident Concha decided she was not about to run when a huge wasp broke up our game of jacks. She stood still, so still the wasp remained on her dark head for what seemed like hours. We stood and watched, thinking perhaps the wasp had mistaken Concha's curly hair for a bush! We watched—and waited.

"*Ujule*, she sure is brave," exclaimed Virgie as she sucked on a popsicle. "She sure is brave."

"She's stupid," grunted Mundo, trying to be indifferent. "She's just a big show-off who thinks she's so big."

"So are you," began Virgie, backing off. "So are you."

"Yeah? Ya wanna make something outta it?"

"Let's go," interrupted Beto in his soft voice. *"Ya vamonos."* He smiled at Concha—who smiled back.

In time the wasp flew away. Concha immediately began to brag about how a "real big wasp" sat on her hair for hours. She never mentioned the ant contest—nor the twenty-first ant that led her to *el lodo*.

You don't feel eleven. Not right away. It takes a few days, weeks even, sometimes even months before you say Eleven when they ask you. And you don't feel smart eleven, not until you're almost twelve. That's the way it is.

—Sandra Cisneros, "Eleven"

ELEVEN

Sandra Cisneros

Sandra Cisneros is an acclaimed fiction writer, essayist, and poet who has worked as a teacher to high school dropouts, a poet-in-the-schools, a college recruiter, and an arts administrator. She has also taught as a visiting writer at a number of universities around the country, as a kind of "migrant professor," at California State University at Chico, the University of California at Berkeley and Irvine, the University of New Mexico, and the University of Michigan. The recipient of two NEA fellowships for poetry and fiction, Cisneros is the author of Woman Hollering Creek and Other Stories *(1991), winner of the Lannan Literary Award (1991), the PEN Center USA West Literary Award (1991), QPB New Voices Award in Fiction (1992), and the Anisfield Wolf Award (1992);* The House on Mango Street *(1984), winner of a Before Columbus Foundation American Book Award (1985);* My Wicked Wicked Ways *(1980; with a new edition in hardcover, 1992).* "Eleven" is from Woman Hollering Creek and Other Stories. *The voices of our childhood begin with those moments Cisneros describes as "all the years inside of me."*

Cisneros says of her writing, "When I was eleven years old in Chicago, teachers thought if you were poor and Mexican you didn't have anything to say. Now I think that what I was put on the

*planet for was to tell these stories. Use what you know to help heal
the pain in your community. We've got to tell our own history. I
am very conscious that I want to write about us so that there is
communication between the cultures. That's political work: making
communication happen between cultures."*

WHAT THEY DON'T UNDERSTAND ABOUT BIRTHDAYS AND WHAT
they never tell you is that when you're eleven, you're also ten,
and nine, and eight, and seven, and six, and five, and four, and
three, and two, and one. And when you wake up on your
eleventh birthday you expect to feel eleven, but you don't. You
open your eyes and everything's just like yesterday, only it's
today. And you don't feel eleven at all. You feel like you're still
ten. And you are—underneath the year that makes you eleven.

Like some days you might say something stupid, and that's
the part of you that's still ten. Or maybe some days you might
need to sit on your mama's lap because you're scared, and that's
the part of you that's five. And maybe one day when you're all
grown up maybe you will need to cry like if you're three, and
that's okay. That's what I tell Mama when she's sad and needs
to cry. Maybe she's feeling three.

Because the way you grow old is kind of like an onion or like
the rings inside a tree trunk or like my little wooden dolls that
fit one inside the other, each year inside the next one. That's
how being eleven years old is.

You don't feel eleven. Not right away. It takes a few days,
weeks even, sometimes even months before you say Eleven
when they ask you. And you don't feel smart eleven, not until
you're almost twelve. That's the way it is.

Only today I wish I didn't have only eleven years rattling
inside me like pennies in a tin Band-Aid box. Today I wish I
was one hundred and two instead of eleven because if I was one
hundred and two I'd have known what to say when Mrs. Price

put the red sweater on my desk. I would've known how to tell her it wasn't mine instead of just sitting there with that look on my face and nothing coming out of my mouth.

"Whose is this?" Mrs. Price says, and she holds the red sweater up in the air for all the class to see. "Whose? It's been sitting in the coatroom for a month."

"Not mine," says everybody. "Not me."

"It has to belong to somebody," Mrs. Price keeps saying, but nobody can remember. It's an ugly sweater with red plastic buttons and a collar and sleeves all stretched out like you could use it for a jump rope. It's maybe a thousand years old and even if it belonged to me I wouldn't say so.

Maybe because I'm skinny, maybe because she doesn't like me, that stupid Sylvia Saldívar says, "I think it belongs to Rachel." An ugly sweater like that, all raggedy and old, but Mrs. Price believes her. Mrs. Price takes the sweater and puts it right on my desk, but when I open my mouth nothing comes out.

"That's not, I don't, you're not . . . Not mine," I finally say in a little voice that was maybe me when I was four.

"Of course it's yours," Mrs. Price says. "I remember you wearing it once." Because she's older and the teacher, she's right and I'm not.

Not mine, not mine, not mine, but Mrs. Price is already turning to page thirty-two, and math problem number four. I don't know why but all of a sudden I'm feeling sick inside, like the part of me that's three wants to come out of my eyes, only I squeeze them shut tight and bite down on my teeth real hard and try to remember today I am eleven, eleven. Mama is making a cake for me for tonight, and when Papa comes home everybody will sing Happy birthday, happy birthday to you.

But when the sick feeling goes away and I open my eyes, the red sweater's still sitting there like a big red mountain. I move the red sweater to the corner of my desk with my ruler. I move my pencil and books and eraser as far from it as possible. I even move my chair a little to the right. Not mine, not mine, not mine.

In my head I'm thinking how long till lunchtime, how long till I can take the red sweater and throw it over the schoolyard fence, or leave it hanging on a parking meter, or bunch it up into a little ball and toss it in the alley. Except when math period ends Mrs. Price says loud and in front of everybody, "Now, Rachel, that's enough," because she sees I've shoved the red sweater to the tippy-tip corner of my desk and it's hanging all over the edge like a waterfall, but I don't care.

"Rachel," Mrs. Price says. She says it like she's getting mad. "You put that sweater on right now and no more nonsense."

"But it's not—"

"Now!" Mrs. Price says.

This is when I wish I wasn't eleven, because all the years inside of me—ten, nine, eight, seven, six, five, four, three, two, and one—are pushing at the back of my eyes when I put one arm through one sleeve of the sweater that smells like cottage cheese, and then the other arm through the other and stand there with my arms apart like if the sweater hurts me and it does, all itchy and full of germs that aren't even mine.

That's when everything I've been holding in since this morning, since when Mrs. Price put the sweater on my desk, finally lets go, and all of a sudden I'm crying in front of everybody. I wish I was invisible but I'm not. I'm eleven and it's my birthday today and I'm crying like I'm three in front of everybody. I put my head down on the desk and bury my face in my stupid clown-sweater arms. My face all hot and spit coming out of my mouth because I can't stop the little animal noises from coming out of me, until there aren't any more tears left in my eyes, and it's just my body shaking like when you have the hiccups, and my whole head hurts like when you drink milk too fast.

But the worst part is right before the bell rings for lunch. That stupid Phyllis Lopez, who is even dumber than Sylvia

Saldívar, says she remembers the red sweater is hers! I take it off right away and give it to her, only Mrs. Price pretends like everything's okay.

Today I'm eleven. There's a cake Mama's making for tonight, and when Papa comes home from work we'll eat it. There'll be candles and presents and everybody will sing Happy birthday, happy birthday to you, Rachel, only it's too late.

I'm eleven today. I'm eleven, ten, nine, eight, seven, six, five, four, three, two, and one, but I wish I was one hundred and two. I wish I was anything but eleven, because I want today to be far away already, far away like a runaway balloon, like a tiny *o* in the sky, so tiny-tiny you have to close your eyes to see it.

"How about it, kid?" asked the man. "I'm giving ya the chance of your life—it's the only way people of your nationality can get ahead."

"I'm an American," said Richard.

". . . Mexicans don't get too much chance to amount to much. You wanna pick prunes the rest of your life?" . . .

—José Antonio Villarreal, from Pocho

from POCHO

José Antonio Villarreal

José Antonio Villarreal's first novel, Pocho (1959), was the first
Chicano novel published by a major publishing company in the
United States. Villarreal was born in Los Angeles, California, in
1910, the wake of the Mexican Revolution. His parents were born
and raised in the state of Sacatecas, Mexico. During the revolution
his father fought in Pancho Villa's army, and in 1921 his family
moved to the U.S., migrating through California as seasonal farm
workers. Villarreal recalls his growing up and the stories he heard
from the migrant community: "And so they talked and told tales of
their region, and I listened. Long into the night I listened until I
dropped off to sleep and my father would pick me up onto his lap as
he continued to talk about the Revolution. . . . And every camp
was different, none existing for more than six or seven weeks, then
off we would go to the next harvest, where new people would
gather and there would be new tales to be told and heard. I knew
when I was six years old that the one thing I most wanted from life
was to be a storyteller."

Pocho is a term used to describe one who is growing up between
cultures. Villarreal's novel describes the experiences of a boy
growing up in Santa Clara and his cultural confusion and painful
encounters with racism. Richard Rubio is the young boy, a pocho,

*who struggles for freedom and a sense of self against the forces of
tradition, conformity, and materialism that surround him. In this
chapter from the novel, Richard Rubio literally fights against those
seeking to route him into work representing stereotypes of the
Mexican American.*

THE WORLD OF RICHARD RUBIO WAS BECOMING TOO MUCH FOR
him. He felt that time was going by him in an overly accelerated
pace, because he was not aware of days but of weeks and, at
times, even months. And he lived in dread that suddenly he
should find himself old and ready to die before he could get
from life the things it owed him. He was approaching his thir-
teenth year, and thought of his friend Joe Pete Manõel, though
not forgotten, did not hurt as much. For the most part, he lost
himself in dreams or spent hours reading everything he could
find, indiscriminate in his choice through his persevering desire
to learn. Now, after work, he was a familiar figure in the town
library, and later, when the vacation ended, he continued the
practice, for by then the meager library at school provided little
for him. Yet he was disturbed by the thought that now, while
he was young and strong in body, his wanderings should be
physical. Imagination would do only when he became old and
incapable of experiencing actual adventure.

At school, Richard was the favorite of his teachers, because
his old-country manners made him most courteous in contrast
to the other students. He was also a good student, and stood
near the top of his class without seemingly trying. His teachers
encouraged his reading, but unfortunately did not direct it, and
he became increasingly complex in his moods.

It was natural that in his frantic hunger for reading he went
through books he did not understand. A friend of his father had
a few Spanish novels, and he read a simplified "Quixote" and

made several attempts at Ibáñez, but for the first time in his life he found reading to be actual work. So he limited his Spanish reading to the newspaper he received in the mail from Los Angeles. With determination, he followed Tom Jones and Dr. Pangloss through their various complicated adventures. From *Gone with the Wind*, he emerged with tremendous respect and sympathy for the South and its people. And when the Dust Bowl families who had begun trickling into the valley arrived in increasing numbers, he was sad. They represented the South to him, and he mourned that the once proud could come to such decay.

When the boy fell asleep over a book, his father blew out the coal-oil lamp and tenderly put him to bed. Only when riding out in the country lanes was Richard forbidden to read. Twice his father threw his books out the window of the car. "Look!" he would say. "Look at the world around you, burro!" And the boy would think, What a funny one the old man is!

Indeed, the father was a paradox.

Richard went into the barn that was used to house the town's garbage wagons. Today the barn was empty of equipment and full of young guys and a few older people. Over at one end of the building stood a huge ring. It had two ropes, instead of three, and the posts were big iron pipes wrapped in burlap. There were two kids going at it pretty hard, and suddenly one of them put his hands to his mouth and stood transfixed in the center of the ring. The other one jumped around, throwing punches that either missed his opponent completely or landed on his shoulders or the top of his head. The puncher was too anxious, and the one who couldn't believe his mouth was bleeding got away, and then the bell rang.

Two other guys jumped into the ring then, and started dancing around and flexing like professionals, blowing snot all over the place, and then this local guy who was doing pretty good in the game up in the City jumped in there to do the announcing, and another guy who was already in there was the referee.

He noticed that the announcer's face was a little bumpy already, and he was already talking through his nose from fighting pro. He was a little guy and he moved around funny—real jerky, like the old silent movies—and somebody said there goes the next flyweight champ, which meant he would be the Filipino champion, since they were the only flyweights around. Richard could tell already he would not even be champ of Santa Clara, but he did not say anything, because people in small towns are funny about things like that—they think they have the best of everything.

While the two guys were fighting, Thomas Nakano came over to him. He was wearing only pants, and they were rolled up to his knees and he was barefooted.

"You gonna fight, Thomas?" asked Ricky.

"I can't find nobody who's my size and wants to fight me," Thomas said, sounding disappointed.

Richard felt his stomach begin to get funny, because he knew what was coming. "Don't look at me, Punchie," he said, trying to make a little joke out of it, but nobody laughed and it was real quiet.

"Aw, come on, Richard." He was begging him to let him hit him. "Come on, you're just my size. I'll fight anybody, only they won't let ya less'n you're the same size as the other guy."

He said no he would not, but he felt sorry for Thomas because he wanted someone to fight with him so bad. And then the guys were finished in the ring, and somboedy called Thomas and asked him if he had a partner yet. He said no, but by then even guys Richard didn't know were trying to talk him into fighting him, and the pro came over, and in the end he was in the ring shaking, because he didn't want any of these people to see him look bad. He thought back to the pictures in *Ring Magazine* and tried to imitate the poses, but before he could really decide which he liked best, Thomas was all over him. He kind of clinched and said, "What the hell you trying to do, you crazy bastard?" And Thomas said, "Don't worry—I'll take it easy," and Richard felt pretty good about then, because Thomas was his buddy and he would take it easy on him. But as they pulled away from each other, Thomas clouted him on the mouth when he wasn't looking, and Richard's head felt suddenly numb. Then Thomas was hitting him all over the place, like nobody's business—in the ribs, the stomach, and even his back sometimes, and the gloves were feeling like great big pillows on Richard's hands. It was the longest round in the history of boxing, and Thomas pissed him off. *My friend—one of the gang!* So he thought and thought, and finally, when they were apart one time, he dropped his hands and moved toward Thomas, looking real sadlike right into his eyes, as if to say, *Go ahead, kill me.* Thomas stopped also, and a funny what-the-hell's-going-on? look came to his face, and when Richard knew he was relaxed good, he brought one up from the next neighborhood and clipped him good right on the ear. Thomas spun clean around and started to walk away; then he walked in a circle and the son of a bitch was smiling, but he walked right past Richard and around the other side again, and all Richard could do was stand there and look at the crooked little legs that were browner than his. Then he heard everybody hollering for him to go after Thomas, and he thought he might as well, so he followed him around, but Thomas wouldn't stand still. So finally he grabbed him and turned him around, and Thomas stood there grinning, and his eyes were almost closed, because his eyelids were almost together anyway. Richard couldn't hit him when he was smiling at him like that. He smiled back at him, and then the bell rang.

Richard couldn't help laughing at Thomas's grin, but suddenly he stopped, because the bell rang again and he knew he was in for it. Right away, Thomas hit him in the stomach, and Richard bent right over, and there it was—he just kept right on going, and landed on his head and took the count there curled up like a fetus. He didn't have to fight any more, and Thomas was very happy as he helped him up, and Thomas kept saying how he was like Fitzsimmons and that his Sunday punch was a right to the solar plexus. "I hit you in the solar plexus, Richard," he said over and over again, but Richard wasn't really listening to him, because he was sneaking looks at the people, and finally decided he had made it look pretty good.

The referee and the professional came over to see him. "Nice faking, kid," said the referee. "How'd ya like to be a fighter?"

"Uh-uh," he said, pulling at the laces with his teeth. The man took his gloves off.

"You don't know how to fight, but you got a punch for a kid and you're smart," he said.

"I not only can't fight, but I'm scared to fight, so you don't want me," he said.

"How old are ya, kid?"

"I'll be thirteen soon."

"I thought you was older," he said. "But, hell, I can teach ya a lot, and in a year I can put you in smokers. Make five or ten bucks a night that way."

"Not me, Mister. I don't need five or ten bucks."

"How about me?" said Thomas. "I'm the guy that won. You saw me hit him in the solar plexus." Now Richard knew why Thomas had been so anxious to fight.

"Yeah, I can use you, too," said the man, "but I want this other kid."

"Oboyoboy!" said Thomas. He had a trade now.

"How about it, kid?" asked the man. "I'm giving ya the chance of your life—it's the only way people of your nationality can get ahead."

"I'm an American," said Richard.

"All right, you know what I mean. Mexicans don't get too much chance to amount to much. You wanna pick prunes the rest of your life?" Richard didn't say anything, and he said,

"Look, I'll go talk it over with your old man, and I'll bet he'll agree with me. I'll bet he knows what's good for you."

"You better not do that, Mister. You don't know my old man. He's already been in jail for knifing three guys."

Richard could tell he was dumb, and, like a lot of people, believed that Mexicans and knives went together. He thought he had finished with him, but the man said, "All right, we won't tell 'im anything, and when you start bringing money home, he'll come and see *me*."

"Listen," Richard said. "He'll come and see you all right, but it won't make any difference. My old man don't feel about money the way some people do. So leave me alone, why don't you?"

But the man kept insisting, and said, "I gotta line up a smoker for the Eagles, and if you and the Jap kid here put 'em on, I'll give ya each a fin. Then, when your old man sees the dough, he'll be in the bag. What do you say?"

"Okay with me," said Thomas, "but don't call me no Jap." Richard was walking away by then, and the man followed him. "I'll give ya seven-fifty and the Jap a fin."

"No, thanks." He kept walking. They would never be able to make him do anything like that. He was sure he could be no more than a punching bag, because, hell, everybody in the neighborhood could beat him, and besides he was afraid.

The guys caught up to him, but he wasn't talking. He thought how funny the guy back there was—the fight manager. He felt that the manager was the kid and he was the grownup. *Amount to something!* Jesus! Everybody was telling him what he should make of himself these days, and they all had the same argument, except that this guy was thinking of himself. At least the little old lady who was so nice and let him read the Horatio Alger books was thinking of him when she told him he should work hard to be a gardener and someday he could work on a rich person's estate; she was sure he would be successful at that, because she had known of some Mexicans who held very fine places like that. . . . Funny about her, how the Horatio Alger books meant as much to her as the Bible meant to Protestants. . . . And the adviser in the high school, who had insisted he take automechanics or welding or some shop course, so that he could have a trade and be in a position to be a good citizen, because he was Mexican, and when he had insisted on preparing himself for college, she had smiled knowingly and said he could try those courses for a week or so, and she would make an exception and let him change his program to what she knew was better for him. She'd been eating crow ever since. What the hell makes people like that, anyway? Always worried about his being Mexican and he never even thought about it, except sometimes, when he was alone, he got kinda funnyproud about it.

As he walked toward home with the guys, he thought about the things he had just discovered. He would never really be afraid again. Like with hitting Thomas and ending the fight the way he did; funny he had never thought about that before—the alternative. Everything had another way to it, if only you looked hard enough, and he would never be ashamed again for doing something against the unwritten code of honor. Codes of honor were really stupid—it amazed him that he had just learned this—and what people thought was honorable was not important, because he was the important guy. No matter what he did and who was affected by his actions, in the end it came back to him and his feelings. He was himself, and everything else was there because he was *himself*, and it wouldn't be there if he were not himself, and then, of course, it wouldn't matter to him. He had the feeling that *being* was important, and he *was*—so he knew that he would never succumb to foolish social pressures again. And if he hurt anyone, it would be only if he had no choice, for he did not have it in him to hurt willingly.

He thought of Thomas's face in the ring, and began to laugh

at the silliness of his grin, and then he laughed louder and louder, about the fight manager and all the people who tried to tell him how to live the good life, and then laughed about the guys with him, because they were laughing like crazy, too, and the sad bastards did not know what the hell they were laughing about.

He was panting and his heart was drumming in his chest. Looking up he saw that the schoolyard was almost empty. Wobbling up the concrete steps, he entered Sister Katherine's classroom. All the students were sitting at their desks; Arturo sat down as Sister Katherine was chalking up the morning's lesson.

Sister Katherine was big; her back was broad and her hips ballooned beneath her black skirt. When she turned around, the rosary she had strung about her neck clicked, jingled, then sent a spark of light into Arturo's eyes. She scanned the class; when she saw that Tony's desk was empty, an ugly scowl appeared on her face. She stood with her arms cradled on her breasts, not saying a word. . . .

—David Nava Monreal, "Sister Katherine"

SISTER KATHERINE
David Nava Monreal

David *Monreal's short stories have appeared in* Seguaro *and* The Bilingual Review/La Revista Bilingüe. *His books include* The New Neighbor and Other Stories *(1987),* Choosing Sides *(1993), and* The Epic Novel *(1993). Because of the prevalence of Catholicism in Mexicano and Chicano cultures, many Chicanas/os share the Catholic school experience. "Sister Katherine" focuses on the relationship between Arturo and his teacher. He vows revenge for her mean-spirited teaching tactics, but his plans are changed. By learning to see beyond even the ugliest emotions—rage, hatred, and prejudice—Arturo is transformed.*

Monreal says of the role of his childhood in this work: "As a young boy growing up in the California central valley, two major things dominated my life. The hot, hot, summers and the tiny wooden Catholic church that sat on the corner of Vine Street and Buena Vista Way. There was never a day that I didn't pass in front of the church, and like all good Catholics, execute that furtive sign of the cross. Even now, thinking of that church brings forth a flood of memories. I think of the sermons and the hymns, I think of the votive candles flickering in their red vases, but mostly I think of the monjas, *those nuns who left their mark on my soul. My writing of 'Sister Katherine' was my attempt at keeping my childhood past alive."*

ARTURO AMBLED DOWN THE RUTTED ROAD THAT PASSED THROUGH
the neighborhood of ramshackle old houses. Out in the front
yards newly washed clothes flapped on the clotheslines and small
kids, not more than three or four years old, were running half-
naked through the parked cars. There was the scent of *huevos y
chorizo* hovering in the morning sunlight and as he passed one
house, weatherworn and battered, he heard the scratchy radio
sounds of Mexican music.

About a hundred yards ahead he could see the wooden
bridge—put together by knotty planks—that spanned the small
neighborhood creek. He walked up to it lugging his school
books under one arm and stood for some long moments studying the scene. There was a bed of stagnant water lying beneath
the bridge, and in the mud flat frogs croaked blissfully. Along
the banks, reeds glistened, butterflies flickered in and out of the
sun and a dragonfly pasted itself to the air.

Arturo moved slowly as he started crossing the bridge whose
wood creaked and swayed. Halfway across he saw a boy bending over the railing, gazing into the water. The boy was slender
and dark and Arturo quickly recognized him as one of his class-
mates, "T-Tony, you're going to be late!"

Tony turned around, "So what?"

"S-Sister Katherine," Arturo stammered, "will get angry."

Tony moved away from the railing and stood next to Arturo.
Tony was a short boy and his long hair fell haphazardly over
his forehead. Just in the way he stood—hands on his hips—he
looked rougher and tougher than Arturo.

Arturo was slightly built; his hair was brown, nearly blonde,
and his cheeks were made rosy by the sunshine. He held his
books with long and feminine fingers.

"I don't care if she gets mad," Tony said looking back into
the water.

"B-But she'll make you say ten Hail Marys."

Tony laughed sardonically. "You're really scared of that old bitch, aren't you? When you talk about her you stammer like a woodpecker. Shit, she don't scare me one bit."

Arturo lowered his eyes in humiliation; he could not help that he was frightened of Sister Katherine. For years he had heard of her reputation as the battle-axe, the female tyrant of Holy Family Catholic School. She was an ugly shrew—flabby arms and thin, black mustache—who ruled her classroom with vengeance. Her voice was so embittered that it could shrivel flowers; now that Arturo was in the eighth grade he had Sister Katherine as his homeroom teacher. He would sit listening to her lectures, but when she turned her glowing eyes on him he would freeze with dread.

"I'm not s-scared of her," Arturo replied.

"Bullshit! I see how you hide your face whenever she looks at you."

Arturo squinted, his pale brown eyes grew watery in the sunlight. "Sh-She's not a bad teacher, sh-she's just trying to help us kids. My m-mother said we should listen to her, we might l-learn something."

Tony smiled; Arturo was a sissy but he couldn't help but like him. "Who really cares what Sister Katherine thinks, she can go to hell." Tony paused, "Well, maybe we better go before you have a heart attack."

The boys left the bridge and began walking the streets. It was warm and the September sun was dropping glittering bits of gold through the treetops. Tony walked swaggeringly, with his hands stuffed in his pockets. He whistled, then at the next corner he spotted the little stand that sold snowcones at five cents apiece. He quickened his pace and Arturo straggled behind him like a kite's tail. After a few moments Arturo realized where Tony was going. "Hey, w-wait a minute, y-you haven't got time for th-that!"

"Says who?"

"Y-You'll be late for sure."

Tony wasn't listening; he ordered a snowcone, then sat in the shade of a tree.

"You've g-got five minutes to m-make it to class," Arturo said glancing at his watch.

"Leave me alone!"

"Y-You're g-going to get into trouble. We're both g-going to get into trouble with S-Sister Katherine."

"Who said you had to wait for me?" Tony moved his hand as though swatting a fly. "Go on, get out of here! Get lost!"

Arturo stood helplessly with his hands dangling at his sides, thinking of Sister Katherine's great looming figure. Then suddenly, without a warning, he bolted down the streets; the wind whistled through his ears as he passed the church. Jumping over a small picket fence, dashing into an alley, dodging an old man setting up trash cans, Arturo made a sharp right near the green wooden house then ran until splotches of perspiration stained his white shirt. Finally reaching the front of the school, he stopped and leaned against the wire fence.

He was panting and his heart was drumming in his chest. Looking up he saw that the schoolyard was almost empty. Wobbling up the concrete steps, he entered Sister Katherine's classroom. All the students were sitting at their desks; Arturo sat down as Sister Katherine was chalking up the morning's lesson.

Sister Katherine was big; her back was broad and her hips ballooned beneath her black skirt. When she turned around, the rosary she had strung about her neck clicked, jingled, then sent a spark of light into Arturo's eyes. She scanned the class; when she saw that Tony's desk was empty, an ugly scowl appeared on her face. She stood with her arms cradled on her breasts, not saying a word.

Arturo shivered; a stream of sweat ran down his chin, then plopped on the desktop. He wondered if Sister Katherine had seen him come in late. He tried to open the book sitting before him but his hands were shaking too much.

"Is there anyone missing today, class?" Sister Katherine boomed.

Everyone in the class craned their necks; their eyes fell on the empty desk.

"Tony Garcia!" They replied.

"How many times is it this week?"

"Three times!"

Sister Katherine's eyes churned with venom. "He has no respect for learning or God!" Color came to her pallid face. "He will be punished this time, I promise you."

The class grew silent, so silent that Arturo knew that his heart was pounding loud enough to be heard. He squirmed in his seat when Sister Katherine turned her eyes on him. *She knows, she knows that I was late but she's not going to do anything about it.*

Tony walked in smiling, he passed the threshold, then stood in front of Sister Katherine. He stood there with one leg cocked and both hands dangling rudely from his pants pockets. Swaying arrogantly, he spoke words edged with defiance.

"I guess I'm late."

A dark cloud passed over Sister Katherine's face, "Yes you are."

Tony shrugged his shoulders.

"And why are you late?"

Tony shot a glance at Arturo, "Because I don't give a damn about this class."

In a blur Sister Katherine's hand rose into the air then came down with brutal force across Tony's mouth. It rose again and came down with even more force; it came down again and again—the whacking sounds of the slaps filled the classroom, and every child witnessing the beating felt a deep fear wash over his heart. They watched as Sister Katherine's hand drew blood from inside Tony's mouth; Tony was in shock, then without even a whimper tears began to roll down his cheeks. Sister Katherine slapped him until his knees buckled and he fell helplessly to the floor.

She stood above him, her face hardened, more impenetrable than granite. She grabbed Tony by the scruff of the neck, hauled him to his feet, then stared straight into his eyes. "Don't ever talk to me that way! Now that God has taught you a lesson!"

She then shoved him down the aisle and Tony staggered to his desk weeping. Arturo felt panic spread through his body, noticing that Sister Katherine had her hands doubled up into fists. *Never, never will I disobey, Sister Katherine, God believe me.*

A month had passed. It was November, and Arturo had been complaining of stomach pains. He would get up early in the morning and spend most of his time in the bathroom. His mother began to worry; she took him to the doctor and after a thorough examination, nothing abnormal was found. But still he complained; one week he missed three days of school, and on the fourth day his mother finally grew angry and forced him to get out of bed. He whined, saying he was sick, and maybe a few weeks away from school would make him feel better. His mother was confused, she couldn't understand how a boy who had done so well in school for so many years could suddenly develop a phobia about attending classes. So she grew concerned and pampered him; she let him stay home and every Thursday she went by the school and picked up his homework. Some of the school-kids inquired about Arturo and the only thing that she could say was that Arturo was sick and not feeling well.

In the meantime Arturo stayed in bed. He played solitaire and did his homework. In the evenings, looking out the window, he could see the sky turn gray with the impending winter. At night he had trouble sleeping—he tossed and turned and had bad dreams. One dream in particular troubled him. He saw himself in an empty classroom taking a test on mathematics; he was struggling with the answers when Sister Katherine walked in wearing an ebony-black habit. She stood above him, hate gleaming in her eyes, and with an emerald-studded crucifix she began to beat him over the head. He took the beating for hours; at last he would awaken screaming, his brow bathed with sweat.

After he had stayed home for three weeks, Arturo's mother decided that it was time for him to go back to school. She packed him a lunch and woke him early in the morning. Arturo tried complaining but nothing that he said would make her change her mind. Reluctantly, he submitted.

He felt sick as he walked to school. It was early December. The clouds were black, and all the leaves had fallen to the ground. A heavy fog had rolled in during the night, and Arturo saw figures moving through the mist like apparitions. When he reached the school he felt a tightening in his stomach; he walked into the courtyard and saw the children playing on the swings. Sitting on a concrete bench, he felt a cold wind blow down his back; pulling his jacket collar over his neck, he saw Tony walking his way. Arturo tried turning his face but it was too late.

"Where have you been, huh? It's almost Christmas." Tony stood above Arturo with his hands stuffed in his pockets.

"I've b-been sick."

"You don't look sick to me."

"B-But I am."

"Make me laugh."

Arturo looked up at Tony, he saw that his nose was red and cold. "It h-had to d-do with my s-stomach." Arturo explained, "I h-had cramps for a long time. The d-doctors s-said that some k-kind of p-parasite was living inside m-my belly."

"No shit?" Tony said raising his eyebrows.

"Yeah."

"I thought that maybe Sister Katherine was making you sick."

Arturo shuddered, "How c-can you s-say that?"

Tony cackled, "I see it in your face."

Arturo rubbed his cold nose with the back of his hand, "H-How has the c-class been?"

"Surviving," Tony said. "What's the matter with your talking?"

"W-What do you mean?"

"You're sounding more like a woodpecker than ever."

Arturo felt himself grow warm with embarrassment. "I d-don't know. M-Maybe I'm n-nervous."

The bell rang and Arturo stood up. He walked with Tony into the classroom. The other kids saw Arturo and suddenly they were overjoyed. They patted Arturo on the back, asked him how he was doing, shook his hand and tried their best to make him feel comfortable. The classroom was stirring when Sister Katherine came in through the front door. Everyone grew quiet; Sister Katherine scanned the room and leaned against the wooden rostrum. She had not changed in the three weeks; her eyes were still cold and bitter, and her stark features had the gleaming hardness of marble. She raised her hands (both of them were gloved) and as she spoke her strident voice pierced the silence.

"Good morning, children."

"Good morning," they replied.

"Today is December third, nineteen sixty-_____ and we have been studying the secular novel entitled *The Grapes of Wrath*. It is a book that documents the Dust Bowl migration. The last time we left off we were reading . . ."

Arturo squirmed in his seat then coughed. Sister Katherine stopped talking, then looked at Arturo. "I see that our sick boy has returned."

Everyone stared at Arturo.

"What was wrong with you? Can you tell us?" Sister Katherine asked.

Arturo hesitated, his ears rang and he felt his face flush. He had his hands lying on his lap and suddenly he could feel them growing wet. Sister Katherine was staring down at him—her eyes did not shift or waver—and she took several steps forward until she stood in front of Arturo's desk.

"I'm sure the class is interested in your disease, Arturo. It may even be educational." Her diction was precise, clear, and there was an imperious grin etched on her face. She waited for Arturo to speak; finally his voice meekly broke the silence.

"I-I-I h-had s-stomach c-cramps."

"Stomach cramps?" Sister Katherine replied.

"Y-Yes."

A sadistic gleam flitted across Sister Katherine's eyes. "I thought only women had cramps."

Arturo turned pale and beads of sweat formed on his upper lip. He didn't know what she meant by that, but he was sure it wasn't good.

Sister Katherine's voice filled the room again, "Have you been doing your homework?"

"Y-Yes."

"Have you been keeping up with your reading?"

Arturo lowered his eyes, "Y-Yes."

"Are you sure?"

He nodded his head, then blinked, her face was too stern and demanding.

"Have you kept up with *The Grapes of Wrath*?"

Arturo trembled. He had been reading the book for three weeks; *why is Sister Katherine picking on me?* "Y-Yes," he replied.

"Then read us the beginning of Chapter Sixteen starting on page two hundred and twenty-two."

Arturo stiffened, not knowing why this woman was being so cruel; she knew that he stammered, that he was sensitive and that he was scared to death of her very presence. But she carried it on as though she were enjoying his torment. Maybe she was sad or mad? He did not know. Maybe she had no one to love her and cruelty was the only way she could express her feelings. Maybe she was lonely? Lonely people did crazy things.

Arturo opened the book sitting on his desk, and, his voice trembling, he held the book in front of his sweating face; slowly his mouth began the ordeal:

"J-Joads and W-Wilsons c-crawled westward as a u-unit. El R-Reno and B-Bridgeport, C-C-Clinton, E-E-Elk City, S-S-S . . ."

He stopped and looked at Sister Katherine; she grinned and planted her feet firmly on the floor, "Go on Arturo, we're all listening."

Arturo went on, hot tears streamed down his face. He heard his stammering fill the room like sad, staccato music. He was trying so hard to say the words correctly, but something inside him—tension, fear—was making it impossible. In the back of his mind he heard some snickering: *I want to die, die.*

When Christmas vacation arrived Arturo thought he would be happy, but he was not. The month had become cold, and every morning a thin blanket of frost would be lying on the front lawn. For one week the rains came, falling in torrents, slicing through the trees, filling up the neighborhood creek and causing the dirt roads to become nothing but slushy swamps of mud. Every day the sky was pitch-black, and whenever Arturo walked to the library he had to wear a wool cap and a thick jacket that made him look twenty pounds heavier than he was. Two days before Christmas he sat in the library reading and rereading the battle scenes of some World War II novel. Reading brought him joy; for hours he could escape the agony of his stutter and the cruel memories of Sister Katherine.

Every afternoon at about three o'clock he would lock himself in his room and listen to his mother talk on the phone. He often wondered why women's voices were shrieky and shrill; maybe it had to do with the fact that all women were banshees and witches. He had felt that way ever since Sister Katherine had humiliated him in front of the class. She had driven a stake in his heart so deeply that now he could not look a woman in the eye. To him they had become the enemy—people to keep away from and all of their perfumes and wily romantic ways were never going to seduce him or make him change his mind. One evening he grabbed his pellet gun and climbed the roof of his house. From there he could see the backyards of every house in the neighborhood; two houses down a family was having a Christmas party in the patio. He saw several girls, dressed up in their frilly best. Without thinking, twice he pumped his pellet gun and shot one of them in the arm. There was yelling and hysterical tears; he sneaked into his room through the window and as he sat on the bed, he laughed and experienced a happiness he never had thought possible.

On Christmas day he opened his present. It was a new shirt from his mother. He put it on, then purposely tore the buttons when he took it off. When his mother offered to sew the buttons back on, he said no: *it was an ugly shirt and he would never wear it again anyway.*

Some nights he would lay awake devising ways of getting even with Sister Katherine. He remembered that Tony had once called her a dyke. He did not know what the word meant; but if he could prove that she was a dyke, maybe he could cause Sister Katherine some pain—yes, pain—and he wanted that ugly, disturbed woman to feel *pain.* One morning while he sat in the kitchen drinking tea the phone rang. When he answered it he heard a familiar voice on the other end. "Arturo?" It asked.

"Y-Yes." He could not believe it but he thought that . . .

"This is Sister Katherine. How has your vacation been?"

His heart thumped—the nerve of that crazy nun. "F-Fine."

"Well I hope so. I want to wish you a Merry Christmas, you and your family. I've been calling everyone in class wishing them the same thing." There was a pause. "Are you still there?"

"Y-Yes."

"Well, anyway, have a fine Christmas, a holy one, and another thing. I forgot to give you all an assignment to be done during the holidays. I want everyone to write a poem, some sort of inspirational poem. When we all get back together, we're going to read them. Do you understand, Arturo?"

"Y-Yes."

"Good. And please enjoy yourself and God bless you. I really do love you children, you know."

Arturo hung up the phone and sat down. He could not believe that he had been talking to Sister Katherine. What was that damn dyke up to? Was she so cruel that she had to call him up just to ruin his holiday, punish him even more?

That night Arturo lay in bed pondering. *What was the reason behind the phone call?* He could not believe that Sister Katherine was in the Christmas spirit and that out of the kindness of her heart she wanted to wish everyone well. The damn shrew had to have a motive. Arturo was going to show her: he was not going to write anything; he was not going to do that assignment she wanted.

Over my dead body.

Around midnight (after experiencing the recurring nightmare) Arturo got up, washed his face, turned on the lamp and began his poem. There were some things that just could not be changed.

Tony and Arturo sat on the concrete bench blowing warmth into their cold hands. The fog had thinned and the school-children ran through the hazy patches of yellow sunlight. Tony yawned then rubbed his eyes. "So she called you too?" he said.

Arturo was wearing his woolen cap, pulled over his ears; tiny diamonds of water glittered on his lashes, "Y-Yeah."

"I wonder why."

"Sh-She wanted to wish everybody a H-Holy Christmas."

"What a bunch of shit."

"Th-That's what I thought."

Tony rubbed his hands against his knees, "She was probably drunk on cheap wine. Every nun and priest drinks on Sunday afternoons. They have orgies in the rectory, you can hear them yelling and screaming."

Arturo's mouth fell, "R-Really?"

Tony grinned, "Nah, but I'm sure they get drunk."

Arturo gazed across the schoolyard, "I wish I c-could find S-Sister Katherine d-drunk. Just once I w-wish I could find her d-doing something wrong. I would report her to the b-bishop, the p-pope."

Tony laughed, "She ain't no saint."

"Th-That's for sure."

"By the way, did you hear?"

Arturo turned his face and saw Tony's black hair fall flatly over his ears, "H-Hear what?"

"About the new nun."

"No, w-what about her?"

"People say she's pretty. Sister Helen got sent back to Los Angeles and this new nun took her place. My dad went to church last Sunday and saw her sitting in the front pew."

"W-What's her name?"

"Elizabeth, yeah that's it, Sister Elizabeth. She's tall and my dad said he saw some blonde hair sticking out of her veil."

"I hope sh-she's n-not mean."

Tony's eyes tightened as he stared at Arturo, "You know that every nun is mean. They ain't ever had a man so they go a little crazy. Do you know what my dad says?"

"W-What?"

"A nun is a woman that ain't had none."

Arturo smiled though he really didn't understand the joke; across the schoolyard a group of kids were gathered in a circle. Arturo looked over, then slowly shifted his eyes on Tony. "D-Did you write your poem? W-What's it about?"

"Nothing."

"C-Come on, tell me."

"It's about a bird, a stupid bird that wakes me up every morning with his goddamn singing."

"M-Mine's about spring."

"Big deal."

"I don't know. It's p-probably lousy. It t-took me t-two hours to write it."

"Shit, I don't care what people think about my poetry, it's for punks anyway."

"I k-kinda like it."

"Yeah, that's 'cause you're a punk."

Arturo sat listening to the schoolchildren laughing. Above the giant oak tree he could see the diffused sun peering through the mist like a full moon on a cloudy night. The children that were gathered in a group kept laughing and giggling; finally Tony stood up and stuffed his hands into his pockets. "What the hell is going on over there?" he said.

"I d-don't know."

Tony climbed on the bench and looked over the milling crowd, "It's the new nun, she's talking with the kids."

Arturo stood up, "Let's go s-see."

"Nah, what for?"

"C-Come on, I want to s-see her."

They gathered up their books and walked across the school-yard. The small kids were crowded around the new nun like gaggles of excited ducks. They kept reaching out and touching her skirt, her elbow. Arturo walked around the kids then broke through the crowd by pushing aside a tall girl wearing glasses. Arturo stood in front of the nun reverently.

She was beautiful; her eyes were blue and her mouth was colored as though with a soft red lipstick. She was tall and slender, her perfectly contoured breasts pressed against the drab looseness of her habit. Her smile was perfect; she laughed musically. She was just too young and pretty to be a nun.

"And who are you?" She said looking at Arturo.

"A-Arturo," he stammered.

"You have lovely eyes, Arturo," she replied.

"Th-Thank you," he sputtered.

"And who's your home-room teacher?"

Arturo felt disgusted as he said the name: "S-Sister Katherine."

The nun faltered, then nervously backed away, "Isn't that nice?"

The children pressed against the beautiful nun; they pushed her towards the third grade classroom. She smiled, patted a few of the children on the head, then disappeared into the building. Arturo stood quite still in the middle of the cold morning, looking at the classroom door that had closed behind the nun.

"Sh-She's pretty," Arturo said.

"Yeah, too pretty to be in this crummy school," Tony replied.

"She said I h-had lovely eyes."

"Maybe she needs glasses."

Arturo felt something tender press at his heart. "I r-really liked her."

"Good. But if we don't get to class, Mrs. Battle-Axe is going to have our asses."

In the classroom Arturo heard nothing; he had fallen into his own private world. He read his history book, but he did not understand a word. During recess he sat on the concrete bench and stared at Sister Elizabeth teaching some girls how to play volleyball. He loved the way she stretched her arms over her head; her voice rang above the children's laughter and once the ball dribbled over to the bench and Sister Elizabeth fetched it gracefully, her eyes beaming, smiling.

In the afternoon the students were reading the poems they had written and Arturo was gazing out the window. The sun had finally dissolved the fog, and the brown earth was being flooded by broken shafts of light. Arturo was feeling dreamy, fragmented—*I'm happy that she liked my eyes*—when a voice broke his reverie.

"Arturo."

Arturo quickly came to his senses; Sister Katherine was standing near his desk.

"Y-Yes?"

"Have you been listening to the poems?"

"Y-Yes, sister."

"How can you be listening to the poems and staring out the window at the same time?"

There was a glissando of laughter, "I d-don't know."

Sister Katherine's voice suddenly softened, "Well, never mind. I think the class would like to hear your poem."

Arturo asked, "D-Do you w-want me to read it?"

"Do you think you can?"

He had to be honest. "N-No."

Sister Katherine smiled. "Well, here then, give it to me."

Arturo was relieved; he handed Sister Katherine the poem, then laid his arms across the desk. He looked up at her; why was she being so kind to him?

Sister Katherine stood in front of the class and began:

> Spring flowers are
> blue,
> like the rain-washed sky.
> The roses drip
> so
> red in the sun.
> I watch everything;
> birds,
> animals,
> fish,
> from the shade.
> So cool, so quiet,
> so peaceful,
> I am in Spring.

Arturo closed his eyes. The poem sounded nice when Sister Katherine read it, but he was sure that it was horrible. He was waiting for the students to snicker, but instead they were quiet. They were showing his poem respect for some unknown reason.

"It was beautiful, Arturo," Sister Katherine said. Arturo was in shock; not once had Sister Katherine said a kind word to him, to anyone for that matter.

"It is an innocent thing of beauty. I like it very much. I think God has given you the gift of poetry." Sister Katherine turned her joyous face to the class, "Children, I think we should all take a lesson from Arturo. The world can be a lovely, precious place if only we look at it in the proper way."

Sister Katherine was changing; every day Arturo noticed something different about her. When she stood in front of the class lecturing, her voice, which was usually a booming intimidating thing, had transformed into a soft, submissive whisper. Even her hands, which were clumsy and coarse, now danced in front of her body like strands of flowing seaweed. As time passed into spring, Sister Katherine's features became more feminine. Though it was against the school's implicit rules, she took to wearing eye shadow and rouge and just before the Easter holiday, she wore a pink-tinted lipstick that for the first time gave her the look of a lady. Whenever she stood near an open window a sweetly scented perfume would exude from her bulky, oversized body.

Arturo was baffled: the woman who had once tormented him was now genuinely interested in his poetic talent. She would read his poems out loud to the class with great feeling and suggest books for him to study. She once took him aside and told him that she had been consulting with a speech therapist and soon she would set up an appointment for him. When spring was in full bloom—flowers were blossoming and peach trees adorned the landscape—Sister Katherine decided that a field trip was in order. The students packed lunches, chartered a bus and headed for the mountains. For an entire day the children were entertained by Sister Katherine; she enthusiastically lectured on botany, geography, natural history and what she called "God's pastoral gift to man." She would sit on a rock with her skirt folded between her legs. On one occasion the class lay in the shade of a giant pine tree while Sister Katherine regaled them with sweet renditions of Bach's recorded music.

The change was so drastic that Arturo did not know what to think. He scratched his head for answers and the only thing he could come up with was that Sister Katherine had gone crazy. He had read that some women, after living without a man for so many years, finally lose their grip on reality. They go on for months as though they were the happiest creatures in the world; then like lightning, they plunge into a deep and irreparable depression. Arturo waited, he waited for Sister Katherine to "plunge." He hoped that he would be there when the dark side of happiness swept her off her feet and into an asylum.

But that change never came; it was the first days of May and Sister Katherine was still wallowing in her ecstasy. She hung religious paintings on the classroom walls and even took guitar lessons so she could sing spiritual songs to her "young and attentive flock." One warm day while Sister Katherine was expounding on poetry, Sister Elizabeth walked in smiling. Her face was lovely and her eyes seemed to reflect the blueness of the sky.

"May I borrow you, Sister, for a minute?"

The class *agreed* and as the nuns stood outside, Arturo could see them talking. They moved their arms about emphatically; a joyous smile hung on Sister Katherine's face as she looked at Sister Elizabeth. They spoke for some long, impassioned moments; then, as though they had dissolved the world around them, they kissed.

Arturo lost his breath, what was that all about? Why had they kissed? He had never seen two women do that before, and for a moment he didn't know what to think. Perhaps it was something they always did after an intimate conversation? It wasn't a deep kiss—more of a peck—but yet, there was something different about the kiss.

When Sister Katherine came back into the classroom her face was flushed with the heat—as she spoke her voice sounded slow, sluggish, like someone who was drowning in a pool of overpowering emotions. Arturo watched her closely: what was that spark, that light radiating from her eyes? During lunch, Arturo sat pensively staring into the cloudless sky. Tony lay next to him, stretched out on the lawn.

"D-Do you know w-what I saw today?" Arturo said.

"What?"

"Y-You w-wouldn't believe me. I saw S-Sister Katherine and S-Sister Elizabeth kiss."

"So?"

"D-Don't you think th-that's funny?"

"Nah, why should it be?"

"T-Two women kissing."

"Nuns kiss all the time. I see them doing it in church, even out in the middle of the schoolground they're holding hands. You can't be that stupid; it has to do with their love of mankind."

"Yeah, but th-this kiss was different."

"How?"

Arturo thought for a second. "I d-don't know, different."

"You're crazy, you know that."

Arturo grew silent. "What's a dyke?"

"Don't tell me you don't know."

"N-No, really, w-what does it mean?"

"What do you think it means?"

"I d-don't kn-know, tell me."

"It means that a woman is a queer, a fag."

"W-What's a fag?"

Tony sternly raised his voice, "You don't know anything, do you? A fag is a queer, somebody who likes their own sex. For instance, if a girl likes going to bed with other girls, that makes her a fag, a dyke, a lesbo."

"S-Sister Elizabeth is a fag."

"Don't talk crazy. She's too pretty."

"If she k-kissed S-Sister Katherine that sh-should make her a fag."

"I explained that to you already. If anybody is a fag, it's that bull-dyke, Sister Katherine."

"Do you think so?"

"Yeah, but I wouldn't spread it around. You could really get people in trouble talking about things like that."

"Y-Yeah?"

"Yeah, and a kiss don't prove nothing."

"B-But the kiss . . . it was s-strange."

"What do you mean?"

"I m-mean they were happy, they were s-smiling. H-Haven't you noticed how S-Sister Katherine has changed ever since S-Sister Elizabeth arrived. I bet th-they're in love w-with each other."

"Don't be stupid."

"I'm s-sure of it."

"So what?"

"I c-can prove it."

"You're just asking for trouble."

"T-Trouble?"

"Yeah, nobody wants faggot nuns teaching in this school."

Arturo's eyes widened, "W-Would they k-kick a nun out for being a dyke?"

"Sure they would."

"I g-got an idea. W-Where do the nuns live?"

"In the rectory."

"Th-The building behind the church?"

"Yeah. What are you getting at?"

"I h-have a plan."

"Don't talk crazy."

Arturo's head pounded—here was his chance to get revenge, to cause trouble for Sister Katherine. He looked at Tony and smiled. Wiping the bread crumbs off his pants, he stood up. *She'll pay for making me miserable, she will.* For a second Arturo felt ten feet tall; a giddy excitement stirred through his body.

"What are you thinking about?"

"I g-gotta go."

"Don't do anything stupid. By next month you'll never see Sister Katherine again."

"I said I g-gotta go."

Arturo walked off through the afternoon crowd; he heard laughing and a distant voice screaming, "You're crazy, Arturo, you really are."

His plan was simple; he would go to the rectory to see the priest, then when he had the chance he would sneak off in search of evidence.

When he knocked on the door an old lady wearing a black dress answered.

"Yes?"

"I'm h-here to see F-Father Martin."

"He's busy at the moment. What does this concern?"

"I'm a s-student at Holy Family Catholic School, and I have some q-questions about my c-confirmation."

The lady smiled, "Come in, you can wait in the foyer."

Arturo sat with his fingers interlocked, he waited for several minutes, enough time to let the woman disappear down the corridor. When the lady was gone, he stood up and walked past a font filled with holy water. He reached a door on the eastern side of the hall, and peeking in, he saw that it was an office; a typewriter sat on an oak desk and a hanging plant swayed above the shuttered window. Walking on further, he saw that at the end of the corridor was a glass door. He could see a courtyard with a garden and a marble fountain spewing water. Opening the door, he walked into the garden. There were flowers everywhere; the fragrance of roses assaulted his nose and a group of hummingbirds flitted about the plants, then quickly slipped over the courtyard wall. He wandered through the courtyard peeking into the windows; there was nothing to be seen but a room occupied with neatly made beds. The courtyard was rectangular and by the time he had peered into every window he was back where he started. The silence was uncanny; above his head he could see splotches of blue sky and up on the gleaming spire two pigeons were preening their feathers. Suddenly there was a noise; it was the delicate, crystal sound of distant laughter. He froze—what if the priest came upon him, what would he say? Hesitantly, he hid behind a pomegranate tree whose fat red bulbs bent the frail limbs. He sat hidden for a long time; the laughter grew louder, then the sound of high-heel shoes clacked against the parquet floor. A door swung open and Sisters Katherine and Elizabeth came flooding into the courtyard; they were wearing dresses and both of them were laughing. They stood in front of the fountain. Arturo held his breath—what was he to do now?

"Lovely morning," Sister Katherine said.

"Yes," Sister Elizabeth replied.

"Did you notice how Father Martin was straining over his Latin?" Sister Katherine paused. "I hear that he was a poor student."

"But the prayer was uplifting," said Sister Elizabeth.

"I can't help but think that he's losing his faith."

Sister Elizabeth was shocked. "How can you say that?"

"It's just the way I feel."

"But you're wrong, the man is just old. We all grow tired as we age."

Sister Katherine turned her eyes on Sister Elizabeth; there was warmth in her curious stare. The women were standing close to each other, and without another word they sat down on a bench. A white light came through the open roof and fell across their faces; they sat quietly, without speaking. Finally, Sister Katherine looked about her, then tactfully, in an elegant gesture, took hold of Sister Elizabeth's hand.

She fondled it and touched the fingertips; she ran her nails over the soft palm.

They sat peacefully: no one would bother them in the garden. Sister Katherine held her face next to Sister Elizabeth's beautiful features. It was a contrast, a study in dissonance and harmony. Sister Katherine touched her lips to Sister Elizabeth's cheek.

"We shouldn't behave like this," Sister Elizabeth said.

"Why not?"

"We could be seen and misunderstood."

"No one comes here in the morning."

"What if someone did?"

"It wouldn't bother me. Who would misunderstand?"

"Many people."

"Pooh on them all," Sister Katherine said.

"We would probably be excommunicated."

"God would still love us. You've got to understand how you've changed me so. Before, I maltreated the children. I was bitter, angry . . ."

"But sometimes I'm so frightened."

"Don't be."

Both women were radiant, strangely, as though this one peculiar moment had transformed them from nuns to humans to lovers. They kissed deeply.

Arturo shuddered; he felt every muscle in his body tighten. All he wanted to do was get away. Gradually he backed up, under the camouflage of the flowers, until he passed through the glass door and was walking down the corridor. He did not know what to make of what he had seen. When he reached the foyer a voice echoed through his head, "My son, wait." The priest was standing near the door.

Arturo stopped but he could not talk.

"Did you need something?" The priest asked.

"S-Sir . . ." Arturo stammered.

"Mrs. Gomez was telling me that you had questions about your confirmation."

Two nuns were in the garden kissing, sir, father, two lesbians are in the rectory making love. Love. Do you understand? "N-No, I haven't any q-questions."

"Any way I can help you, my son, feel free to ask."

"N-No, I've changed my m-mind."

"What is your name, my son?"

"A-Arturo Castro, father."

"Yes, I've heard about you. You're that Mexican poet Sister Katherine often speaks about."

"Sir, I have to g-go."

"What is the hurry?"

Running out the door, into the sunlight, Arturo ran down the block until his chest nearly burst. Crossing the old bridge (not noticing the two naked children trolling for tadpoles), running and running and jumping a fence until he squatted beneath the shade of a walnut tree. He sat there for hours. Sparrows trilled in the branches. Butterflies gyrated wildly in the air. He sobbed . . . sighed . . . held his breath for a long, painful moment. He knew a secret. He would never forget. Love changes everyone . . . even Sister Katherine.

As the weeks passed, Sister Katherine completed her transformation. She organized a small party for the graduating class, and while everyone was drinking tea and eating cake she recited several of Arturo's poems. On confirmation day she was there, standing close to beautiful Sister Elizabeth, greeting and directing the milling congregation. Arturo's mother attended the ceremony and was overjoyed by Sister Katherine's kindness.

Sister Katherine was aglow as she extended her hand to Arturo's mother. "Mrs. Castro, your son is a poet, a true, natural poet."

Arturo stood there listening. He was wearing a black suit and bright white tie. The sun was hot and as he turned to look at Sister Katherine's face, the radiant light hurt his eyes.

PASSAGES:
WE WHO ARE
NOT AS OTHERS

Divorce. Like a faceless statistic, the word should have simply died in the air. But in a conservative Texas town, in a Chicano neighborhood, the word was anathema. For lower-class, churchgoing Chicanos in 1963, divorce meant scandal; and my parents' divorce—ironically a surprise to us children, furtively planned and consummated—had just gone through. . . .

—Thelma Reyna, "Una Edad Muy Tierna, M'ija"

UNA EDAD MUY TIERNA, M'IJA

Thelma Reyna

Thelma Reyna was born in a small town in Texas and spent most of her childhood there. She presently lives in Pasadena, California. She is a school administrator and the author of short stories and poetry that have appeared in journals, including Voices *and* El Grito del Sol. *In "Una Edad Muy Tierna, M'ija," a horribly unsettling divorce traps a fifteen-year-old between her feelings for her parents and her own growing sense of self. The author says of the relation of her writings to her life: "Almost everything I have published is an account of something straight out of my childhood. My family life was turbulent, even though I generally consider my childhood to have been a happy one. One of my favorite brothers was killed in Vietnam at the age of eighteen, a loss that my mother never really overcame. Both of my maternal grandparents, who were very dear to me, died during my adolescence or early adulthood. Therefore, loss was a reality that colored many of my perceptions about growing up, and it was an inevitable companion to love. Oftentimes, I weep when I compose a story or poem, because, as I write it, I relive it, complete with all the pain and sorrow that attended it. It seems, unfortunately, that the events most filling my 'writing mind' are painful ones."*

IS THERE A GOOD PLACE TO HIDE, I WONDERED AS I WALKED THE dusty road of my neighborhood. The caliche of our unpaved street powdered my ankles gray. I didn't care. Ordinarily, I would mumble my displeasure as I'd stumble among the larger chunks of gravel, but on that particular day the street could have been a swami's spiked bed for all I cared.

The spikes were in my heart. My father had told me I was at a very tender age—*una edad muy tierna, m'ija*, not long after a particularly violent argument between him and my mother. I'd been caught in the middle, used as an alibi by them both, questioned by both, their jealous distrust of each other building to a crescendo until I'd run outside in tears.

My parents' marriage was crumbling—ugly, vermin-eaten framework crumbling, rotting. For years, pieces had been chipping off in personality clashes, in marathon arguments that outdistanced midnight and heralded daylight without shame. And always, we children—nine of us in varying degrees of involvement, with varying degrees of comprehension—had pleaded heroically with them to stop, or had wept helplessly, or hid, or innocently sought refuge with TV or games in sympathetic neighbors' homes. We older ones (I was second oldest, eldest daughter) had struggled with passionate involvement in their conflicts, or with sanity-maintaining apathy; shame that our calmer neighbors knew all too well the loud discord within our home, or defensive bitterness toward the busybody bastards with their horribly-disjointed noses; and the most heart-rending ambivalence of all: see-saw love and hate for our thirtyish, handsome, turbulent parents.

Es edad muy tierna, m'ija. Fifteen. *And I'm so sorry that you're going through all this*. He'd been unable to hide his own tears that day, and I knew he knew better than I the resentment boiling just under my skin. We were all living in hell.

Through my wet eyes now, I glanced to left and right and wondered how many of the neighbors were watching me as I plodded skinnily down the street. I walked quickly, my pigeon feet unfocused as I watched them almost tripping. I glanced from house to passing house, wondering, wondering. Do they know? wishing, wishing that a rut in the corduroy street would suddenly yawn and take me into it, out of this hell, maybe into Hell itself. Houses with neighbors I'd never met and even those kindly ones I'd known metamorphosed suddenly into cells of malice. I heard the neighbors' whisperings in the dusty silence: "Look. There she goes, the poor child. Yes, yes. Have you heard? Bebe and Raul have divorced."

Divorce. Like a faceless statistic, the word should have simply died in the air. But in a conservative Texas town, in a Chicano neighborhood, the word was anathema. For lower-class, churchgoing Chicanos in 1963, divorce meant scandal; and my parents' divorce—ironically a surprise to us children, furtively planned and consummated—had just gone through.

The whispered scandals skipped from mouth to mouth in each alien house I passed: "Did you hear Bebe and Raul fighting last night? Did you know he left?" My neighbors were omniscient bastards! "It was the worst one yet. He had to go. She divorced him, and he didn't even know. Can you believe that?" My tears streamed silently. "He had to go. The police were there." Then, in a conspiratorial hush my heart heard: "Were you the one who called them?"

Sudden red light pulsating against the living room wall. Authoritative knock on the screen door. Red noise. When I'd gone to the door, the two policemen's bulk blocked out the porch light. Who called them? They squeezed into the narrow hallway, looking for my father.

"Where is he?"

Who called them? Which of our good neighbors called the police on my father again? Let us have hell in this house in peace!

I hurried to the rear hallway while the policemen boomed their questions at my weeping mother in the living room. In the hallway my father was also weeping. Half-dressed, he knelt on the floor and hugged my small brothers tightly, stammering reassurances nobody understood. Five children in the hallway, five small children surrounding a manchild sobbing wildly, saying goodbye to a family he did not know when he'd see again. In the living room: the police voices, my mother's confusion. And in the darkness of the alley, I saw my half-naked father run toward his car. His slight figure shrunk to nothing in the near-blackness, and I prayed my thanks to God that his car finally started, finally tugged away just as the policemen's boots thundered toward where I stood on the back porch.

Goodbye, dear father, goodbyegoodbye. You've left a burning home, father. You've left your share of tonight's violent, vulgar words hanging in the air here. You left a few tufts of hair on the floor where mother pulled them out in rage. We hate you we love you we're glad you're gone so maybe now we can have peace but come back come back come back dear father.

I watched the thin clouds of caliche dust rise about my ankles. I'd left school early that day, for who can concentrate on books when life intrudes? All morning a gray plug had blocked my throat. Child of scandal, child of hate. Why hadn't I sprung forth from man and woman bound so tightly in love, that they became manwoman instead? What was it in a union that chafed and wore the bonds until love whimpered away to nothingness?

I gasped. I'd seen fire and spring, ugliness and filth and radiance in my father, in my mother. How many times had my whimpers of disappointment and fear—yes, hate, too—filled my room? I'd whimpered, but my love for them had never whimpered itself into nonexistence.

Child of hate, child of love.

I stopped suddenly in the street and faced the small, nondescript houses ranged opposite me. I looked from one to the other and nodded slowly.

"Yes, yes. Child of love, do you hear me?" I waited for an

answer. A fifteen-year-old scandal waited in the dust. No faces showed in windows. No figures sat on front porches. No busy neighbors walked the street or watered anemic flowers.

"Yes, yes. Do you hear me?" I waited in the hot silence and allowed the tears to flow. I was a child again, a more-child child. Memories flowed.

"I'm a child of love, do you hear?" I shouted. "He used to love her, damn it! He told me once she was like a lily to him on their wedding night. She was the first woman he ever knew, and he *knew* her for twenty years!"

Twenty years.

The tears flowed. My defiance was still mute, but I knew the world could hear. I knew as I stood under the sultry sky that day that the world watched. In a supreme, salving effort, my subconscious choked out scene after scene which had been pushed to the back rows of my memory. There *had* been loving times! These had been almost obliterated, and the thought that misery could wipe away joy so easily shamed me more deeply than my parents' present scandal.

The film my mind played back flashed on a giant screen, there in the loneliness of midday:

My mother's hands routinely grooming him: trimming his thick, reddish-brown mustache, clipping the hairs in his nose and ears gently. He gazed at her steadily in her aqua chenille robe, placed his hands on her hips or breasts occasionally. She gossiped nonchalantly as he sang or teased . . .

The film whirred:

He arranged her red negligee so it hung over her legs and over the edge of the couch more smoothly, then stepped back to catch the pose. Her black, immaculate hairdo was perfect, queenly, for this private cheesecake photo session. They didn't know we sneaked a look . . .

Scene after scene flashed:

My father's voice, thin but urgent, his hands tugging on the telephone cord: "I want the doctor now!" His voice pushed itself onto the other party. "I think the baby's coming any minute!" Red face— red with impatience, with pride, with joy. Worry and excitement as keen about his ninth child as with his first.

My mother, bundled in the softest blanket he could find, carried as precious luggage to the car. My weary father returning home only after his ninth child, his seventh son, was born.

The film whirred smoothly, endlessly. "Yes, yes. Child of love." *(He lay in their narrow bed and rubbed her inner thighs.)* They loved each other. *(As he rubbed, he sang to her a song he made up about the white silkiness of her skin.)* He loved my mother! *(She smiled at him, then he told us children to go outside and play.)*

I no longer shouted. I didn't need to hide. My terribly misguided parents had been manwoman once. For twenty years, their union had been love/hate. The ultimate scandal last night, incredibly, had been love, too—gasping, distorted, on its knees, love not flawless as it once was, but love in its nadir.

It could not have been anything less.

I, Salomon, tell you this so that you may know the meaning of life and death. How well I know it now, how clear are the events of the day I killed the giant river turtle. Since that day I have been a story-teller, forced by the order of my destiny to reveal my story. I speak to tell you how the killing became a horror. . . .

—Rudolfo Anaya, "Salomon's Story" from *Tortuga*

SALOMON'S STORY

from *TORTUGA*

Rudolfo Anaya

Rudolfo Anaya is a professor in the Department of Languages and Literature at the University of New Mexico, and one of the most prolific and acclaimed Chicano short story writers and novelists. Among his novels are Bless Me, Ultima *(1972),* The Silence of the Llano *(1982),* Heart of Aztlán *(1976),* Tortuga *(1979), and* Albuquerque *(1992; winner of the 1993 PEN Center USA West Literary Award). His nonfiction books include, among others, his coedited* Aztlán: Essays on the Chicano Homeland *(1989) and* A Chicano in China *(1986). This selection from* Tortuga *tells the story of a boy who is injured in a near-fatal accident and must wear a full body cast, which earns him the nickname of Tortuga (Turtle). Salomon is a* curandero, *a paralytic mute who communicates with Tortuga telepathically. Salomon introduces the boy Tortuga to Tortuga Mountain, a place of* agua bendita *(holy water) that has curative power. Salomon tells Tortuga of the mysterious healing found in the power of storytelling. Anaya says of this work: "The story reflects my growing up along the river and the fishing and hunting that we used to do as kids. Later on in life, reflecting on that aspect of our nature as hunters, I realized that we had done some things wrong. I also learned that the relationship between the hunter and the animal that is hunted is very special, and I learned that from my friend who was a man from Taos Pueblo.''*

BEFORE I CAME HERE I WAS A HUNTER, BUT THAT WAS LONG AGO. Still, it was in the pursuit of the hunt that I came face to face with my destiny. This is my story.

We called ourselves a tribe and we spent our time hunting and fishing along the river. For young boys that was a great adventure. Each morning I stole away from my father's home to meet my fellow hunters by the river. My father was a farmer who planted corn on the hills bordering the river. He was a good man. He kept the ritual of the seasons, marked the path of the sun and the moon across the sky, and he prayed each day that the order of things not be disturbed.

He did his duty and tried to teach me about the rhythm in the weather and the seasons, but a wild urge in my blood drove me from him. I went willingly to join the tribe along the river. The call of the hunt was exciting, and daily the slaughter of the animals with the smell of blood drove us deeper and deeper into the dark river. I became a member of the tribe, and I forgot the fields of my father. We hunted birds with our crude weapons and battered to death stray raccoons and rabbits. Then we skinned the animals and filled the air with the smoke of roasting meat. The tribe was pleased with me and welcomed me as a hunter. They prepared for my initiation.

I, Salomon, tell you this so that you may know the meaning of life and death. How well I know it now, how clear are the events of the day I killed the giant river turtle. Since that day I have been a storyteller, forced by the order of my destiny to reveal my story. I speak to tell you how the killing became a horror.

The silence of the river was heavier than usual that day. The heat stuck to our sweating skin like a sticky syrup and the insects sucked our blood. Our half-naked bodies moved like shadows in the brush. Those ahead and behind me whispered from time to time, complaining that we were lost and suggesting that we turn back. I said nothing, it was the day of my initiation, I could not speak. There had been a fight at camp the night before and the bad feelings still lingered. But we hunted anyway, there was nothing else to do. We were compelled to hunt in the dark shadows of the river. Some days the spirit for the hunt was not good, fellow hunters quarreled over small things, and still we had to start early at daybreak to begin the long day's journey which would not bring us out until sunset.

In the branches above us the bird cries were sharp and frightful. More than once the leader lifted his arm and the line froze, ready for action. The humid air was tense. Somewhere to my left I heard the river murmur as it swept south, and for the first time the dissatisfaction which had been building within me surfaced. I cursed the oppressive darkness and wished I was free of it. I thought of my father walking in the sunlight of his green fields, and I wished I was with him. But it was not so; I owed the tribe my allegiance. Today I would become a full member. I would kill the first animal we encountered.

We moved farther than usual into unknown territory, hacking away at the thick underbrush; behind me I heard murmurs of dissension. Some wanted to turn back, others wanted to rest on the warm sandbars of the river, still others wanted to finish the argument which had started the night before. My father had given me an amulet to wear and he had instructed me on the hunt, and this made the leader jealous. Some argued that I could wear the amulet, while others said no. In the end the jealous leader tore it from my neck and said that I would have to face my initiation alone.

I was thinking about how poorly prepared I was and how my father had tried to help, when the leader raised his arm and sounded the alarm. A friend behind me whispered that if we were in luck there would be a deer drinking at the river. No one had ever killed a deer in the memory of our tribe. We held our breath and waited, then the leader motioned and I moved forward to see. There in the middle of the narrow path lay the biggest tortoise any of us had ever seen. It was a huge monster which had crawled out of the dark river to lay its eggs in the warm sand. I felt a shiver, and when I breathed the taste of copper drained in my mouth and settled in my queasy stomach.

The giant turtle lifted its huge head and looked at us with dull, glintless eyes. The tribe drew back. Only I remained facing the monster from the water. Its slimy head dripped with bright green algae. It hissed a warning. It had come out of the water to lay its eggs, now it had to return to the river. Wet, leathery eggs, fresh from the laying, clung to its webbed feet, and as it moved forward it crushed them into the sand. Its gray shell was dry, dulled by the sun, encrusted with dead parasites and green growth; it needed the water.

"Kill it!" the leader cried, and at the same time the hunting horn sounded its too-rou which echoed down the valley. Ah, its call was so sad and mournful I can hear it today as I tell my story. . . . Listen, Tortuga, it is now I know that at that time I could have forsaken my initiation and denounced the darkness and insanity that urged us to the never-ending hunt. I had not listened to my father's words. The time was not right.

"The knife," the leader called, and the knife of the tribe was passed forward, then slipped into my hand. The huge turtle lumbered forward. I could not speak. In fear I raised the knife and brought it down with all my might. Oh, I prayed to no gods, but since then how often I have wished that I could undo what I did. One blow severed the giant turtle's head. One clean blow and the head rolled in the sand as the reptilian body reared back, gushing green slime. The tribe cheered and pressed forward. They were as surprised as I was that the kill had been so swift and clean. We had hunted smaller tortoises before and we knew that once they retreated into their shells it took hours to kill them. Then knives and spears had to be poked into the holes and the turtle had to be turned on its back so the tedious task of cutting the softer underside could begin. But now I had beheaded the giant turtle with one blow.

"There will be enough meat for the entire tribe," one of the boys cried. He speared the head and held it aloft for everyone to see. I could only look at the dead turtle that lay quivering on the sand, its death urine and green blood staining the damp earth.

"He has passed his test," the leader shouted, "he did not need the amulet of his father. We will clean the shell and it will be his shield! And he shall now be called the man who slew the turtle!"

The tribe cheered, and for a moment I bathed in my glory. The fear left me, and so did the desire to be with my father on the harsh hills where he cultivated his fields of corn. He had been wrong; I could trust the tribe and its magic. Then someone shouted and we turned to see the turtle struggling toward us. It reared up, exposing the gaping hole where the head had been, then it charged, surprisingly swift for its huge size. Even without its head it crawled toward the river. The tribe fell back in panic.

"Kill it!" the leader shouted, "Kill it before it reaches the water! If it escapes into the water it will grow two heads and return to haunt us!"

I understood what he meant. If the creature reached the safety of the water it would live again, and it would become one more of the ghosts that lurked along our never-ending path. Now there was nothing I could do but stand my ground and finish the killing. I struck at it until the knife broke on its hard shell, and still the turtle rumbled toward the water, pushing me back. Terror and fear made me fall on the sand and grab it with my bare hands. Grunting and gasping for breath I dug my bare feet into the sand. I slipped one hand into the dark, bleeding hole where the head had been and with the other I grabbed its huge feet. I struggled to turn it on its back and rob it of its strength, but I couldn't. Its dark instinct for the water and the pull of death were stronger than my fear and desperation. I grunted and cursed as its claws cut into my arms and legs. The brush shook with our violent thrashing as we rolled down the bank towards the river. Even mortally wounded it was too strong for me. At the edge of the river, it broke free from me and plunged into the water, trailing frothy blood and bile as it disappeared into the gurgling waters.

Covered with turtle's blood, I stood numb and trembling. As I watched it disappear into the dark waters of the river, I knew I had done a wrong. Instead of conquering my fear, I had created another shadow which would return to haunt us. I turned and looked at my companions; they trembled with fright.

"You have failed us," the leader whispered. "You have angered the river gods." He raised his talisman, a stick on which hung chicken feathers, dried juniper berries and the rattler of a snake we had killed in the spring, and he waved it in front of me to ward off the curse. Then they withdrew in silence and vanished into the dark brush, leaving me alone on that stygian bank.

Oh, I wish I could tell you how lonely I felt. I cried for the turtle to return so I could finish the kill, or return its life, but the force of my destiny was already set and that was not to be. I understand that now. That is why I tell you my story. I left the river, free of the tribe, but unclean and smelling of death.

That night the bad dreams came, and then the paralysis. . . .

I don't pretend to know when my love affair with Comstock began, but whatever I feel for this town has everything to do with Francisco Ruelas Guerrero, my mother's father. Because of him, a blue horse flew across the early sky of my childhood imagination, and a world of ancient voices sang to me in his garden of blue light. For a child of eight discovering the world, he had just the right magic. It is healthy for a child to have heroes, but I worshipped him and knew enough about him on which to build a dream. . . . As I said, I was a hopeless dreamer, and Grandpa believed in dreams. . . .

—Olivia Castellano, Prologue for *The Comstock Journals*
(or *Sotol City Blues*)

PROLOGUE FOR
THE COMSTOCK JOURNALS
(OR *SOTOL CITY BLUES*)

Olivia Castellano

O livia Castellano *is a professor of Chicano literature and writing at California State University at Sacramento. She has completed three books of poetry:* Blue Mandolin: Yellow Field *(1980),* Blue Horse of Madness *(1983), and* Spaces That Time Missed *(1986). Her fourth book of poetry is a work entitled* For Women: Thank God the Moon Is Forgiving. *She says of her growing up:* "Comstock, Texas, is the fictitious country I carry in my head. It is a little pueblo that I've lifted from the yellow bleak terrain of South Texas and that has come to symbolize my defiance of history, my refusal to be destroyed by my borderlands childhood. Whenever I write, I always return to that particular piece of land and sky, my aesthetic space that gives me the necessary energy to believe in myself as a Chicana and as a poet." *The following excerpt from Castellano's first novel in progress,* The Comstock Journals, *charts the relationship of a young girl to her family and her country.*

A FEW YEARS BACK, IF ANYONE HAD TOLD ME YOU COULD FIND comfort in the memory of a town, I would have thought them insane. If they had said that on the brink of madness what can keep you from falling over the edge would be the memory of a town and a girl who believed in magic—I would not have believed them.

But through the years, this is what has happened to me with Comstock, an insignificant southwest Tex-Mex border town where I lived as a girl, trapped between earth and sky for what seemed an eternity. To escape, I invented a blue garden and a horse with enormous wings. Comstock was already an old woman about to die. Yet, because she knew I was a dreamer, she held me in her arms away from hurt and let me dream in a time when everything was uncertain and dreams were all you could ever be sure of.

It is vanity to think your childhood town special. But what you take from a place you must in some way give back. Because in its final hour, a town gathers itself in and reclaims its own, or at least those who remained faithful in spirit. It pulls back everything it once gave life to. A town remembers everything. And in the final analysis, when you have to settle accounts, you must pay back.

I have not tried to hold on to Comstock; it has held on to me. In my deepest delirium the voices I heard were the same ones I heard in Grandpa's garden and the song they sang was his favorite: "En el cielo, en la tierra, en el mar; en la tumba estaremos los dos."

Whenever I close my eyes, I see a girl and an old man walking hand in hand in early evening, a bright orange moon behind them. They are crossing a wide open plain—yellow dust on their bare feet and the wind in their hair. For a second, they are happy. Then they turn to see their mad pursuers—a madman with ropes around his waist, brujas laughing and wearing white chiffon dresses, women with butcher knives high in the air ready to strike—and the girl and the old man break into a run. This image comes in dreams or when the night is quiet.

Grandpa Francisco Ruelas Guerrero lies buried in the cemetery just beyond the last railroad crossing between Comstock and Del Rio. Uncle Manuel of the Ropes died a model patient in a mental hospital in San Antonio; the brujas too are dead, and the aunts of the butcher knives take pills to control the urge to kill. I have tried in small ways to appease their ghosts, have written poems to them and sang them songs. But this has not been enough.

I have been more faithful to Comstock than I planned. She let me live each day believing life was good and God was everywhere in her yellow, bleak terrain. Because of her, the earth was magic and the sky for dreamers. She lived in all of us, but only I believed in her. It is only natural she chose me to dream her into today.

Whenever things got too sad or complex for my eight-year-old heart, I would stand in front of our house and look in all directions. I would hook my eyes at the horizon and sink into the small ocean of earth and sky that was Comstock. At a young age, I learned to define myself by becoming the space I inhabited. I willed myself into her landscape, defining myself by the Rio Grande to the south, la barranca and Devil's River to the northeast, and the Pecos to the west.

As I grew, I realized the world was a larger place, and limitless in terms of the spaces we could become. Soon, Comstock was not enough. To escape I invented a winged horse, blue horse of dreams, that I could ride high above south Texas to see what else I could be. The horse became a necessary dream. I didn't know then that it was all deception because there is no escape from that first country we shape as children, first enchantment with earth and sky, which we carry with us and touches everything we are to do and become.

Someone once said that in memory everything happens to music. Comstock has become a singular song. In the face of memory, the heart and mind become a willing theatre. This is when you come to accept fully that a town lives on inside you. You look down from a lighting booth onto a huge bare stage washed in blue light. Slowly, you hear dogs barking, a girl singing a sad refrain ("En el cielo, en la tierra, en el mar . . ."). And they begin arriving. First, Grandpa Francisco and Odilia—he is an old man, gray hair and mustache; brown skin and high Tarascan cheekbones. He wears blue coveralls, steel-toe work boots, and a dirty hat. And she a thin girl of eight, her face bright, eyes large and inquisitive; hair in braids and her dress, blue gingham plaid with a large white collar and a bow tied in back. Then comes her mother, Remedios the simple, soft-spoken woman, slender and dark with eyes like the girl's. Next, Uncle Manuel, hair standing on end as if some monstrosity keeps him perpetually frightened, his eyes wide and penetrating. Wearing khaki pants and shirt, he walks nervously as if many voices are calling from all directions. Others follow—aunts, uncles, brothers, sisters, fathers, niños, viejitos—toda la gente de Comstock. They arrive bewildered and dusty, having trekked across the wide yellow desert of memory and onto the stage of praise, hoping to be perfected in remembrance. The year is 1955; Odilia Magallanes is eight years old again. This is how I see them—again and again. Their memory follows me everywhere.

I don't pretend to know when my love affair with Comstock began, but whatever I feel for this town has everything to do with Francisco Ruelas Guerrero, my mother's father. Because of him, a blue horse flew across the early sky of my childhood imagination, and a world of ancient voices sang to me in his garden of blue light. For a child of eight discovering the world, he had just the right magic. It is healthy for a child to have heroes, but I worshipped him and knew enough about him on which to build a dream. Through the years and the slow unravelling of painful truths, I have come to see him as a man. But truth has not destroyed him in the heart where memories live. As I said, I was a hopeless dreamer, and Grandpa believed in dreams.

Later, in my grown-up bouts with madness, I came to doubt every nook and cranny of my existence. At times, I have even doubted whether Grandpa and Comstock ever existed. This is why I must tell their story—to confirm once and for all that they did exist. The grandfather I knew as a child was as real as the one I later discovered—who tried to kill his wife for her infidelities.

But, when you have held on to memory for so long, no new revelation must be allowed to change certain facts. Grandpa taught me to fly with my eyes and listen to voices. As long as I had faith, he said, I would be able to fly. In summer, he taught me to pray to the hot desert sand in the name of the Apache and Comanche blood spilled on those plains. These are facts a child holds on to. He showed me how to search for ominous red lights that hid among the chaparrales at night. He said they were the evil of money which Spaniards had taken away from the Indians and hidden, money and gold burning in their own red hell. And wherever a light landed, a buried treasure was to be found. Yet, one time he and a friend dug where a light had signalled. All night they dug, about seven feet deep, but all they found was a crate full of worms. Grandpa said his friend's jealousy had turned the treasure into evil.

And at night, he taught me to scan the sky for omens, falling stars and flashing lights—signs of birth and death, he'd say. Every time Grandpa saw a strange light in the sky, a child was born or someone died. Grandpa and Comstock had a secret link. So, whatever life Comstock had translated itself to me through him. He had become Comstock. Town and old man were one. As a child I knew this; as an adult, it took years to understand and accept. Children have a way of knowing things in their blood. And, if you are lucky, one day that special knowledge finds you—the words come to lie down on your skin or whisper in your ear. It took a long time for the words to find me.

It happened on the brink of insanity, in the delirium of self-destruction. Years of running away from myself, rebelling against everything I had become had led me into the black hole of a total breakdown out of which I almost didn't crawl. I had subconsciously tried to kill the child I had been. The brown, dusty Mexican girl who grew up in a racist southern town had come to hate what she had become. She tried to deny that she came from a long line of Mexican peasants and illiterates, that she had been spat on and called "dirty Meskin" so many times she knew the curl of a racist's lips just before the words were mouthed.

To compensate for self-hate, I had become obsessed with playing girl-wonder and trying to be all things to everyone else except myself. These acts of self-deception and self-hatred had led me to an insane nightmare-filled depression accompanied by a hopeless case of self-pity, total physical fatigue, and hallucinations. All I know is that one morning, at age twenty-six, I woke up unable to get out of bed or make sense of the world around me. I remained this way for one year. My parents refused to hospitalize me. I am sure if they had, diagnosis would have been borderline schizophrenia, which, once inside, would have blossomed into classic paranoia. Thank God, mine have always been a hardy people who took care of their own locos and misfits.

I, who had made promises to Grandpa that I would someday be a teacher and a poet, was now rotting in a bed, unable to make a simple phone call without falling apart or hold down a clerical job, though a master's degree in literature hung on my wall. I would go to sleep at night praying death would find me before morning; during the day, I would gaze into space, trying to erase myself.

One morning, about three or four months into the madness, I looked at the clock and realized its hands and numbers were incomprehensible and meaningless. "What time is it?" I asked my sister. "It is eleven in the morning," she said. But I had no notion what that meant. Time—like my life—had become irrelevant and illogical. Soon, in similar fashion, the names of days and months lost meaning. I could not even recall their names, much less list them in order. The boundaries of conventional reality were quickly giving way. Food and liquid inevitably landed on my chest as I lost track of the borders of my own body, of where space ended and my body began. I had started to fuse into emptiness.

A few weeks later, the whispering began. Such incredible whispering—like many voices of people on a telephone all talking at once or like a powerful recitation delivered in stage whispers by a huge chorus; at other times, it was more muffled, like when you put your ear to the locked door of a room where many people are conspiring against you.

One singular thought hit me: once I allowed myself to understand the voices, there would be no salvation. They would begin controlling, would command me to cross to the other side from which—once I crossed over—there would be no return. One day, I clearly made out the phrases, ". . . because you know she said . . ." and, "let me tell you about her . . ." A growing fear gripped me: they were talking about me! I felt persecuted by gossipmongers who were spreading horrible gossip about me. Hallucinations of being dismembered by these voices and my bones left to rot on an open field began to haunt me. But, strangely enough, they also angered me. And thanks to my anger, I began a conscious effort to fight back. Whenever I sensed the voices coming, which usually began with a buzzing in the right ear which hit at any time, in broad daylight or in the deep dark night, I would drag myself to the bathroom or kitchen sink and splash cold water on my face, shaking my head from side to side as violently as my limited strength allowed. In the beginning, this would keep the whispering at bay. But, soon, the voices came more often and the whispering intensified. I could no longer make them stop.

"Dear God," I said to myself, "do I really hate myself this much? Is this how I want to end up—sitting in some mental ward talking to myself? Or worse, doing terrible things to others or myself at the command of some voice or devil of my own making?" With the voices came faces. Of this, I was certain. I had visions of becoming like my poor Uncle Manuel in Comstock, who, about an hour before an epileptic seizure hit him, would become a raving maniac; he'd talk to imaginary people, complain that faces were laughing at him and look for something or someone to destroy.

Strange. Now that death wearing the mask of insanity was knocking at my door, I wanted more than ever to live. I, who had hated myself, my past, my peasant origins, wanted to live. But, since everything inside me had already been erased—sense of self, love of family, sense of history and time—nothing was left to pry me from the grip of this madness. It became clear to me that to fight these voices and win, I would have to reinvent myself, to go far back to the waters of childhood.

The first chance available, I called my mother and my sister together and pleaded, "Please, tell me everything you can remember about Comstock." At first they tried to humor me by bringing up little incidents—how we picked wild strawberries (pitayas) en el monte behind the old schoolhouse and would get home looking like payasas, our faces smeared with the purple juice. Or how we'd go for long walks along the railroad tracks and stop to steal El Pollito's roses. He was an elderly man with white hair who lived alone by the railroad crossing and was thin and frail like a fragile little chicken—when he'd finally see us scurrying around his yard cutting flowers, he'd say, "Ustaydes, mushashas, qweren aqua?" We'd run, carrying the flowers in the lifted skirts of our dresses.

Soon talk shifted on to Grandpa Francisco, how happy we felt whenever he gazed upon us, how important and whole in his eyes. The more they reminisced, the more that Comstock began to sift into me with its yellow, dusty plains and blue open-armed sky—all began to shift and rearrange itself, slowly and crudely at first, like a collage of pictures drawn by very young children.

With all their generosity of spirit, my mother and sister—in the tradition of good raconteurs—began to weave a blanket of remembrance. And then, literally, as I gained strength, my sister Viviane would wrap a blanket around me and take me for long drives in the country. I would stare at the Sacramento River and its trees, begging them to come inside me. I needed to learn to see and feel again; but everything flitted by fast or in slow motion—trees, cars, houses—all exaggerated.

In the following weeks, the more they talked of Comstock, the more its yellow earth and blue horizon sifted into memory's eye. And as my past cleared, so did the present. Memories of earlier trees made these new trees more meaningful. Whenever I sensed the whispering coming, I would will myself into memories of Comstock, splashing them quickly on the disoriented canvas in my mind, using the palette of incidents my mother and sister were providing. "Comstock, where are you? Please help me!" I'd say whenever I heard a trace of whispering building up inside. With my eyes shut tight, I would pray with every cell in my body, every imagined ridge in my brain. And, sure enough, Comstock would come keening—its yellows and blues pounding on my eyelids. Being able to will myself into time past made me less fearful of the present. Also, the montage of past images somehow interfered with the whispering, reduced it to a mournful humming or a simple ringing in the ear. This continued for a long time, a battle of voices: the one of memory and the other of God knows what demons which were trying to build their house in my head.

Finally, one morning toward the end of this one-year journey into self-effacement I went to wash my face, and as I bent down over the bathroom sink I heard for the first time the voice of memory: a gentle feeling crawled up the back of my legs from the soles of my feet, and I felt a warm breath on my shoulders, as if someone were standing directly behind me. Then, I clearly recognized my grandfather's voice. "Hija," it said, "your time has not come. Do as you must before you lie down to rest." His soothing words, like small, warm hands, were lightly pressing on my upper arms. So palpably real was his presence that when I looked into the mirror, I expected to see Grandpa standing behind me though he had been dead twenty years. Alas, I was alone. Yet, for the first time in a year, I felt the corners of my mouth curling up in a smile. And, for the first time, I willed my own tears. I cried because a girl was standing in an open field, calling my name, "Odilia! Odilia!" Gently, she was calling, and an old man was coming to lead her by the hand. The two were walking home together once again. I stood like that for what seemed an eternity—peaceful, wonderful eternity—reliving entire scenes of the childhood I had spent with my grandfather. When I opened my eyes, Mother was knocking at the bathroom door, calling my name, asking if I was all right.

I knew at that moment that memory can sneak up and rescue us when we least expect it, and if we're lucky, we'll be ready when she comes. For the first time, I accepted that we are what we have been; to run away from that truth is to drive the self insane.

At year's end, I began a frenzied effort to recollect everything I could about Grandpa and Comstock. It was hopeless, because I was trying to remember as a little girl would recall her childhood town, much as I had done with my mother and sister's help. That particular Comstock had died for me long ago. What I really needed to recall was the Comstock that through the years had become Grandpa Francisco, the town layered with my own life.

It's the same as when you love someone through many years of joy and pain. Whenever you gaze at that person's face, it is no longer just one face but the layers of faces you have known and loved in that one person through the years. You see, Comstock is not just a town where I, Odilia Magallanes, lived as a girl and knew an old man who loved me beyond myself. It is many towns, the layers of memory itself, of the years that passed me while I held on to, destroyed, and rediscovered a girl, an old man, and an old woman named Comstock. It is layered with the knowledge that, in the face of time, memory and madness are at constant war. Do you see why I don't really know when this love affair began? We suffuse things we love with the essence of ourselves so that they no longer have a life of their own. In many ways, I have become Comstock; it has no life other than the one I give it. Too much has happened between us for someone else to tell her story. It is all vanity, a hopeless lover's possessiveness of a hopelessly unreal beloved.

Do you see, then, why I tread gently as I go back to my pathetic little group of peasants and illiterates whom I have learned to love? I must show them as they were before and after Time, the incredible magus with all the aces up his sleeve, tried to destroy them for me; and before Love, master of deception, distorted them in the deepest heart of memory. I must show them as insanity tried to use their voices against me.

I want to say simply that they lived, through everything— poor uneducated "Meskins," my people—heroic, brown, tragic and beautiful; they lived with hope because to have given up would have been against God, against life. They lived with all the humility they could muster in their collective ignorance. Now, in all their violence and sorrow, they live on, tied right here to me. I need to say, finally, this is where it all began, and I can put it all to rest. These are the sandy plains where a girl could draw strength from the mesquites and chaparral.

Comstock, when I lived there as a child, was a dreary, lonely place where one could get close to nature's mystery. The wind moaned and dust devils danced around us. It is about fifteen miles from the Rio Grande to the south, and about the same distance from the Pecos River on the west. Devil's River is to the northeast. The ground was both blessed and cursed long before my clan crossed its horizon. We lived so isolated that to survive we befriended the howling wind and yellow earth. Originally, its name was Sotol City, named for the sotol plant that grew in huge clusters everywhere. A piece of land nestled by three rivers had its own enchantment. But for me, it was

Grandpa who made it fertile in the heart. In my earliest recollection, he was always there. And, whenever he gazed upon me or laid a gentle hand upon my head, the open plains and clear blue sky were one.

When the power of the earth reaches you through the love of a pure-spirited old man, you are twice blessed. Sometimes, however, I think the town and the old man knew all this would come to pass—that I would become obsessed with their memory, that they invented me, and dreamed me into the future simply to tell their story. I have no other life I can call my own. Conspiracy of memory and madness—Comstock, Grandpa, and I handcuffed through eternity. Toda mi gente de Comstock lie buried in the old cemetery next to the last railroad crossing on the road to Del Rio. All chose to be buried in the bowels of Comstock as if to say, "You made sure life would not defeat us, time would not forget us; now we offer ourselves to you."

Once I tell their story, everything can settle down and come to rest, undisturbed through the yellow sands of time, until someday, somewhere, a child not yet born will grow to tell the story of another town, another magical old man. To have this hope is to know finally in your heart that God exists. We can say, "Oh, let me tell you this or that story." But what we really mean is, "Let me tell you how I came to learn God lives, how a town and an old man taught me to love and give life, to bring out the dead and let them breathe again."

Going up and down the block was one thing, but taking the first curve, out of sight of Mom and the house, was another. I was scared of riding on Sarah Street. Mom said hungry dogs lived on that street, and red anger lived in their eyes. Their throats were hard with extra bones from biting kids on bikes . . .

—Gary Soto, "The Bike" from *A Summer Life*

THE BIKE

from *A SUMMER LIFE*

Gary Soto

Gary Soto is the author of eight poetry collections, including A
Fire in My Hands *(1990) and* Black Hair *(1985), the essay
collection* A Summer Life *(1990), two books of occasional essays,
and the prose memoir* Living Up the Street *(1985) for which he
received a Before Columbus Foundation American Book Award
(1985). He is also the editor of* Pieces of the Heart *(1993), and
the much-acclaimed anthology* California Childhood *(1988). Soto
has received the Discovery-*The Nation *Prize, and U.S. Award of
the International Poetry Forum, in addition to fellowships from the
Guggenheim Foundation, the National Endowment for the Arts,
and the California Arts Council. His works for children and young
adults include* Baseball in April, *a collection of short stories about
young people growing up in California's San Joaquin Valley,*
Taking Sides, Pacific Crossing, *and* Local News. The Pool
Party, *one of the short films he has produced, was awarded the
Andrew Carnegie Medal for Excellence in Children's Video
(1993).*

*"The Bike," which is the subject of another Soto short film, is
from* A Summer Life *and tells of a five-year-old boy's bravado
when he defies his mother to leave the confines of his yard for the
forbidden Sarah Street. Soto says of his childhood: "I was a*

*playground kid. I jumped at every chance to play, and jumped on
every borrowed bike from the neighborhood. I also liked swimming
in the public pool, and I dreamed of tossing myself head first into
the ocean. I finally did so when I was thirteen, and rode the waves
until my eyes were blood red and every muscle in my body was
exhausted."*

My FIRST BIKE GOT ME NOWHERE, THOUGH THE SHADOW I CAST
as I pedaled raced along my side. The leaves of bird-filled trees
stirred a warm breeze and litter scuttled out of the way. Our
orange cats looked on from the fence, their tails up like antennas.
I opened my mouth, and wind tickled the back of my throat.
When I squinted, I could see past the end of the block. My hair
flicked like black fire, and I thought I was pretty cool riding up
and down the block, age five, in my brother's hand-me-down
shirt.

Going up and down the block was one thing, but taking the
first curve, out of sight of Mom and the house, was another. I
was scared of riding on Sarah Street. Mom said hungry dogs
lived on that street, and red anger lived in their eyes. Their
throats were hard with extra bones from biting kids on bikes,
she said.

But I took the corner anyway. I didn't believe Mom. Once
she had said that pointing at rainbows caused freckles, and after
a rain had moved in and drenched the streets, after the sparrows
flitted onto the lawn, a rainbow washed over the junkyard and
reached the dark barrels of Coleman pickle. I stood at the window, looking out, amazed and devious, with the devilish horns
of my butch haircut standing up. From behind the window, I
let my finger slowly uncurl like a bean plant rising from earth.
I uncurled it, then curled it back and made a fist. I should
remember this day, I told myself.

I pedaled my squeaky bike around the curve onto Sarah Street, but returned immediately. I braked and looked back at where I had gone. My face was hot, my hair sweaty, but nothing scary seemed to happen. The street had looked like our street: parked cars, tall trees, a sprinkler hissing on a lawn, and an old woman bending over her garden. I started again, and again I rode the curve, my eyes open as wide as they could go. After a few circle eights I returned to our street. There ain't no dogs, I told myself. I began to think that maybe this was like one of those false rainbow warnings.

I turned my bike around and rode a few times in front of our house, just in case Mom was looking for me. I called out, "Hi Mom. I haven't gone anywhere." I saw her face in the window, curlers piled high, and she waved a dish towel at me. I waved back, and when she disappeared, I again tore my bike around the curve onto Sarah Street. I was free. The wind flicked my hair and cooled my ears. I did figure eights, rode up the curbs and onto lawns, bumped into trees, and rode over a garden hose a hundred times because I liked the way the water sprang up from the sprinkler after the pressure of my tires. I stopped when I saw a kid my age come down a porch. His machinery for getting around was a tricycle. Big baby, I thought, and said, "You can run over my leg with your trike if you want." I laid down on the sidewalk, and the kid, with fingers in his mouth, said, "OK."

He backed up and slowly, like a tank, advanced. I folded my arms behind my head and watched a jay swoop by with what looked like a cracker in its beak, when the tire climbed over my ankle and sparks of pain cut through my skin. I sat up quickly, my eyes flinging tears like a sprinkler.

The boy asked, "Did it hurt?"

"No," I said, almost crying.

The kid could see that it did. He could see my face strain to hold back a sob, two tears dropping like dimes into the dust.

He pedaled away on his bucket of bolts and tossed it on his front lawn. He looked back before climbing the stairs and disappeared into the house.

I pulled up my pants leg. My ankle was purple, large and hot, and the skin was flaked like wood shavings. I patted spit onto it and laid back down. I cried because no one was around, the tears stirring up a lather on my dirty face. I rose to my feet and walked around, trying to make the ankle feel better. I got on my bicycle and pedaled mostly with the good leg. The few tears still on my eyelashes evaporated as I rode. I realized I would live. I did nothing fancy on the way home, no figure eights, no wiggling of the handlebars, no hands in my pockets, no closed eye moments.

Then the sudden bark of a dog scared me, and my pants leg fed into the chain, the bike coming to an immediate stop. I tugged at the cuff, gnashed and oil-black, until ripping sounds made me quit trying. I fell to the ground, bike and all, and let the tears lather my face again. I then dragged the bike home with the pants leg in the chain. There was nothing to do except lie in the dirt because Mom saw me round the corner from Sarah Street. I lay down when she came out with the belt, and I didn't blame the dog or that stupid rainbow.

Carlos soon became the king's apprentice. Most of the time the lessons were fun and easy. The hard part was in seeing the same things the king saw. The gargoyles always hid, and the gnomes seemed to appear only in dark places where all they did was giggle. The king would laugh and say you had to try looking for these creatures in a special way, you had to concentrate and maybe catch them off-guard. . . .

—Ron Arias, "The Castle"

THE CASTLE

Ron Arias

Ron Arias, a writer and a journalist for People magazine, is best known for his highly acclaimed novel The Road to Tamazunchale (1975), a story in the tradition of magical realism. He is a winner of the University of California, Irvine, Chicano Literary Contest. He was raised in central Los Angeles in and around the neighborhood of Lincoln Heights. "The Castle" is about the secret doorways and hidden tunnels we discover in childhood that show us the passages from childhood games to visions of ourselves in an adult world. Arias writes: "The 'castle' referred to in the story actually existed and has now been replaced by Woodrow Wilson High School on a hill overlooking central L.A. That hill was a place my friends and I would use as our playground, our escape. It also served as a later inspiration for my fiction."

LISA SCREAMED WHEN THEY TOLD HER CARLOS WAS PLAYING WITH a tarantula in the middle of the street. She ran across the lawn, and when she struck and yanked him onto the sidewalk he refused to cry.

Then the tarantula began hopping. The children backed away, and a gangly boy with red hair said he would go get his father.

"¡Válgame dios!" Lisa muttered, pushing her son toward the front porch and wincing at her sciatica pain. "If only your father were here. . . ."

The man in the pickup shouted for everyone to stay back, and as he shifted into second gear the right-front tire missed the small, hairy mound by inches. Suddenly the tires stopped and began to turn the other way. The children—silent, bending their heads to see beneath the truck—heard the squish. Carlos squeezed his mother's hand and closed his eyes. The man then removed a shovel from the back of the pickup and carefully scraped the wet, flattened mass from the asphalt.

"Idiota," Lisa said, "it could've killed you."

Carlos would not open his eyes. "No it couldn't. It just wanted to get across the street."

"Vente," she said and led him into the house, down the hallway and to his room. His punishment was to stay in his room until she called him for lunch.

For a while Carlos lay in his bed with his head under the pillow and thought how nice it would have been if the tarantula had lived. He was still playing with the animal, letting it touch the stick, nudging it, coaxing it across the street. He knew he would play until his mother's pain had stopped; then she would call him and they would eat lunch together.

Lisa lit her cigarette with nervous hands. The kitchen was stuffy, the reflection on the white table hurt her eyes. Removing her sunglasses from the apron pocket, Lisa again begged her husband to return. A prisoner of war for three years, he knew nothing of the problems at home, the car accident, her sciatica, the monotony, the silence of the house, the scares Carlos gave her, knew nothing of the effort to wake in the morning, to speak, to smile, to keep the house as it was, ready for his return. *Carlitos, your daddy went away, but he'll be back. It won't be long. . . .*

And to fill the emptiness, to make it seem her husband was gone for a few days, for only a few weeks or months, Lisa assumed nothing would change, not even Carlos. For almost a year she would not cut the boy's hair. She let it grow long and curly, despite what the other children said. Then on the day she received the missing-in-action telegram, she told the barber to clip it so it wouldn't look messy. "Daddy wants you looking like a boy," she had said, collecting what fell to the floor and placing it in a large manila envelope.

"Mommy, is he coming home?"

Lisa glanced at the barber, then asked her son if he would like to write his father a letter. "You can tell him all about your new teacher and about the picnic in Elysian Park."

Carlos nodded and watched his mother rub her eyes as if she were trying not to see something. Even then he sensed his father would not be home for a long time, since letters always took weeks to come and go.

Gradually Carlos discovered he could look for his father in his own way. It was only a game, but it was more fun than waiting for letters that never came.

Often after school he would find his mother in bed, fully clothed, reading her books in the wan afternoon light. Or she would be pulling weeds by the oleander bushes that bordered the backyard. Or listening to her Mexican records in the cool darkness of the den, sometimes crying. Carlos would take her hand and say, "Daddy's coming home, he'll be back"—remembering only his father's cologne, the adenoidal laugh and his soft, kinky-wool polo shirt, reminded only by the many photographs and their nightly rosaries asking God to bring him home.

"Mijito, go take your nap," Lisa would say, and Carlos would run to his room, close the door and change into his hidden clothes. He called them his daddy's clothes, and he used them only when he went into the hills to look for his father. He would put the pillow, his football and pajamas under the blanket so she wouldn't notice he was gone, then slip out the side door of his bedroom, close it quietly and tiptoe along the side of the house.

Now, as the hour passed and the tarantula disappeared across the street, Carlos worried that his mother might forget to call him. Leaving his bed, he opened the door slightly and peeked into the hallway. His mother was talking to someone, but it wasn't like telephone talk. Carlos shuffled to the kitchen, hoping she would hear him. "Mommy?" he whispered.

"Sí, mijito," she said without realizing she had spoken. She was staring at the open page of her diary.

"Can I come out now?"

Lisa turned, her long black hair dropping over her blouse. "You know what you did. Go back to your room."

"But it's Saturday."

"Stay in your room till I tell you."

"But . . ."

"Ándale! What if that thing had bit you? What would your daddy say?"

Carlos went to his room and sat on the edge of the bed. His father wouldn't mind. His father liked spiders and snakes and dark places. He wouldn't have punished him.

Carlos opened the blinds and felt the warm sunlight on his forearms. The roses were in bloom, and he could smell the jasmine beneath the windowsill. His temples swelled, his skin grew tiny bumps like football leather, and finally he decided to leave. Maybe she would forget him, maybe she wouldn't call him until dinnertime.

He hurried. He knew Sam would be waiting in their castle on top of the hill.

Carlos leaned into the dry wind as he rushed up the slope at the end of the block. Beyond the dead-end was an even steeper climb. He leaped over the weeds in the ditch and headed into the tall, yellow-brown grass. He hoped the others weren't there, especially the redheaded kid who chased him into the tunnel the first time he had gone to the castle. He remembered the tunnel had been cool and hollow sounding. Later, when he found Sam, the old man said it was the best place to be on a hot day. But you had to be careful where you stepped. Animals would bite only when you bothered them. But Carlitos didn't know that then; he only knew the redhead and the others were outside waiting for him. So he crept forward following the shafts of light that came through the small windows of one wall.

". . . the boogieman's gonna eat you!"

"Hey, Charlie! He's gonna eat you like an enchilada!"

"Come on back! We ain't gonna hurt you. . . ."

The voices echoed, pushing him blindly, making him stumble. Then something moved in the dark. Carlos stepped back, but the voices again pushed him forward. It seemed they were right behind him. "The devil's in there! He's gonna get yoooooou, yoooou, yoou. . . ."

At the end of the tunnel he turned to the left, and now the light came through jagged holes in the ceiling. It was warmer, and he could see the fallen chunks of concrete and twisted metal rods on the floor. The voices were gone. He continued to the end of the passage and again turned to the left. Trailing one arm along the concrete wall, he stumbled forward, now crying, thinking he was walking down into the Earth. Then he tripped on Sam.

"Who's that?" the old man said, pulling his legs back and sitting up. "Well, who are you? Speak up!" He bent over the small figure on the floor.

"Carlos," the boy said.

"Carlos?" Sam said, trying out the name. "Carlos, this ain't no sidewalk. This here's my bedroom. Actually, my bedchamber. And ya don't come in without knocking first."

"Yes . . . yessir."

"Now, what ya here for?"

"They're chasing me."

"Who is?"

"Those guys outside."

"Well, don't you worry. They ain't never comin' in here, they always stay up on top. You stay here a while, they'll be goin' pretty soon."

"I gotta get home, sir. My mom will be looking for me."

"Stop cryin'. Only fools cry." The sunlight tipped his long, white hair, and Carlos drew back from the darkened face.

"Who are you?" Carlos asked after he had stopped crying.

"Sam, king of this castle."

"You're not the devil?"

"That's what they told ya, didn't they? They told ya that so ya wouldn't come down here. Well, now ya know, I ain't the devil."

Carlos was silent.

"Take my hand," Sam said, and Carlos touched, then held the bony fingers. They walked in the direction Carlos had come from. "Watch your step," Sam said. "These rocks keep the marauders from comin' in." He pointed to a stairway cluttered with debris. "You go up on top and make a run for it . . . and don't fall into no traps. I got them all over the castle roof." For a moment the boy was unable to move. Then he felt the old man's hand on his back. "Only fools get caught, and ya ain't no fool, Carlos. Get up there and show them how ya ain't afraid."

Since that time Carlos refused to cry.

For weeks he and Sam would spend their brief afternoons together on the tower, on the battlements or on the courtyard wall, counting houses or cars, standing guard or planning defenses against attack. And Sam would use strange words—marauders, parapet, fortification, forage. Once Carlos found him in the east dungeon peeling a grapefruit. Sam had just returned from an expedition to the tracks.

"I'll get you some forage from my house," Carlos offered.

But Sam refused. "Wouldn't be right. A king gives charity, he never gets it. . . ."

Carlos soon became the king's apprentice. Most of the time

the lessons were fun and easy. The hard part was in seeing the same things the king saw. The gargoyles always hid, and the gnomes seemed to appear only in dark places where all they did was giggle. The king would laugh and say you had to try looking for these creatures in a special way, you had to concentrate and maybe catch them off-guard. Carlos squinted, he shielded his eyes, he looked out of the corners of his eyes, he closed his eyes, he blinked, finally he gave up and said he might have seen them.

The king's lectures began wherever they happened to be. "Don't ya believe in dragons," he said while balancing himself above the royal toilet. "Ain't no such thing, Carlos. That's only in fairy tales. . . . Could ya give me the newspaper now. . . ."

But the tigers, the marauders and an occasional black knight would visit the castle. For some reason the king would always forget his plans for defense, and he and his apprentice would hurry to the arena stairs and descend into the cool safety of the bedchamber.

"Mommy, what's that place on top of the hill?" Carlos once asked Lisa as she stooped by a pile of leaves in the front yard.

"Don't you go up there," she said.

"What is it?"

"It was going to be a country club . . . for movie stars. But they ran out of money and stopped building it." Lisa dropped the rake. "Help me put the leaves in the basket, then maybe we can go to the plunge."

"Do country clubs have plunges?"

"Pools, mijito, swimming pools."

Carlos looked up at the castle. That's why it goes down at one end. But why does it have a tunnel around the sides? Sam says the marauders use the arena to fight in . . . but how come I never see them? Maybe if I look through my fingers like he does, maybe next time I'll see them. . . .

"Carlos! Don't just stand there. Put the leaves in the basket."

One time as Carlos was stacking rocks along the open side of the courtyard, the king asked him if his mother knew about the castle. "Does she know you're here?"

"She thinks I'm in bed taking my nap."

"Maybe ya oughta tell her."

"Naw, she wouldn't like it. She's afraid I might get hurt, then my daddy would get mad."

"Hey, show me which house ya live in."

"That one, see . . . the white one on the corner."

"Got your own room?"

"Yeah, but she makes me play in the garage. She says I'll mess things up in the house for when my dad comes home."

"Where's he?"

"In the war. She says he's a prisoner, and he'll be back when it's over."

For a long while they were quiet. Then the king took a deep breath and tipped his imaginary crown to the boy. "Just remember, ya always got your castle. . . . Yeah, it's yours too."

Now, as Carlos crawled over the dry earth, reaching for handholds on the steepest, uppermost part of the castle hill, he heard the voices. He looked below, at the house on the corner, and hoped his mother would not call him for lunch, that she would forget, that she would not call him until dinnertime.

Loose clods of hardened dirt rolled between his legs, bouncing, disappearing into the grass. Again the voices. He searched the hillside, trying the many ways of seeing what he had not seen before. The wind, thick with heat and the smell of sage, beat down the grass to form waves and slick little eddies where rabbits and birds could lie. He couldn't tell whether the voices were near or far, for the wind would bring them clearly, then suddenly push them away.

He reached the castle wall, climbed through a hole and as he stood beneath the tower, he could hear the king's voice, shouting, and the king never shouted. Only when fighting, and Carlos had never seen him fight.

Crouching low, Carlos moved past the broken courtyard tiles and slipped through the servants' quarters. He listened. They were in the arena. Then he heard the king cry out as if he had been hurt. Carlos shimmied up a pipe to the platform surrounding the arena, clambered over the top, and crawled to the inner edge.

In the far, deep corner was the cowering figure of the king, curled up with his hands over his face. The redhead and four other boys were jabbing him with sticks. "Come on, you faker! Scare us now! Come on, you ole wino. . . ." The boys laughed, then picked up rocks and began to hit the jibbering target on the ground. Finally someone suggested they drop him from up above.

"Naw, it might kill him."

"How 'bout pissing on him?"

"Hey, let's get a snake. . . ."

While they were talking, the king lifted himself on one knee. The redhead threw another rock, missing, then turned to look behind. "Better think of something or—"

Carlos lay still.

"Hold it," the redhead said. "Look who's here."

"Run, Carlos, run!" the king shouted.

"Shut up!" and a large rock hit the old man on the chin.

"Hey, come on down!" another boy yelled. "Don't you wanna hit the devil?"

"Leave him alone!" Carlos shouted angrily. He ran along the top of the arena and glared down at the marauders. "Leave him alone!"

"Look who's giving orders," the redhead said. The others laughed.

"This is our place, get out of here!"

"Make us." The redhead motioned to the other boys and

before Carlos could step back, they threw their rocks. The small figure on top slumped to the concrete and began kicking wildly.

"Let's go," the redhead ordered, "we got him good."

"What about the old man?" one of the boys asked.

"Forget him, he ain't worth the trouble."

Carlos pitched from side to side, kicking and screaming. The small hands beat the ground, and the dark blood spilled off his face like an egg with a broken yolk.

"What happened to ya, boy? Move your hand away . . . easy, take it easy. . . . It's me, Sam."

Carlos lay in the king's arms as the stooped figure hobbled over the parapet and dropped into the shadow of the castle.

At the white house on the corner, the king knocked on the door. Some of the blood around the socket was dry, but the other eye was still wet with tears.

Lisa opened the door.

"Your boy's hurt," the old man said. He couldn't say more.

Later, when the ambulance arrived, when Carlos had been given a shot for his pain, when his mother had forgotten hers, when the king looked down on the boy's bandaged face, Carlos said very quietly that he had seen the marauders. Then he clutched the cold, bony fingers. "We'll get them. . . ."

The old man still couldn't speak.

"Mommy?"

"Sí, mijito."

"Okay if I help Sam? He might get hurt."

"Carlos," the king said finally, "you do like your mother says."

"Please, Mommy?"

"We'll see . . . maybe when your daddy comes home."

Lisa climbed into the ambulance next to her son, the door was closed, and Sam, stepping back, wondered if the castle would be there when the boy returned.

It was at this cafeteria I was first looked at as a women, or so I imagined. Flirting with a young man over my fried fish filet, I felt him looking at me as well. Burning with embarrassment, I turned away, attempting to ignore him, and when I looked up, he was gone.

Later on, I wondered if I'd really had this exchange or not. I was in my teens, skinny-chested, wild-eyed, with a thick mop of unruly curly hair, straddled on either side by two imposing women, my mother and her sister. Could a look have gotten through? . . .
—Denise Chávez, "The McCoy Hotel"

THE MCCOY HOTEL

Denise Chávez

Denise Chávez, *widely praised writer, was an assistant professor
at the University of Houston and is currently teaching at New
Mexico State University, Las Cruces. A native of Las Cruces,
New Mexico, she is a playwright, actress, and fiction writer and
has presented workshops in theater and writing throughout the
United States. She has also toured a one-woman show based on her
writings entitled* Women in the State of Grace. *Seventeen of her
plays for adults and children have been produced throughout the
United States and abroad. She is author of numerous and diverse
works, including a collection of dramatic short stories,* The Last of
the Menu Girls *(1986); a novel,* Face of an Angel *(which will
be published in 1994); a children's play in Spanish,* The Woman
Who Knew the Language of the Animals *(1993).*

*"The McCoy Hotel" is a place where a single mother of three
and her daughters come together for a period of respite. But as in
many of the other stories in this anthology, their meeting place holds
a symbolism much deeper than mere location. It is a site of cultural
memory, a location for a vision of self. Chávez says of this story:
"I grew up in a very small town in the desert. To be able to go to
the big city, El Paso, and see the hope, the excitement, the
possibility for transformation, was very important. My mother,*

*sisters, and I did get together at the McCoy Hotel. The story is
about that transformation of place, the longing and the magic of
youth."*

HERE'S YOUR KEY, MRS. CHÁVEZ. MRS. MADRID IS IN 417.

The elderly clerk handed the usual key to my mother. Room
415. The McCoy Hotel. El Paso, Texas.

It was a key that signified so much to the women in our
family. To my mother this key was a grateful respite from
her duties as a third grade teacher, a divorced mother of three
children, two of us still at home.

When she had this key there was no rushing to her charges,
no small children crowding around, waiting to be soothed.
There was no return to feverish midday meals or anxious waits
for that long awaited child-support check, the one that never
came.

My mother's everyday worries disappeared on those days at
the McCoy Hotel. Her life there was not like her other life,
which was always rushed, and filled with disappointment and
disillusionment.

My mother's days started with early morning mass after
which she would return home to get us out of bed and make
our breakfast. Oatmeal was what we ate every day; there was
never any change. My sister, Margo, and I always left our
oatmeal untouched, complaining about its texture. It was always cold, lumpy as well and could literally be lifted out of the
saucepan like an unbroken grey mold.

Time not having improved its taste, and barely noticing it,
mother would eat the oatmeal hours later, sitting in front of the
television set during her lunch break from school, her keen ears
tuned to the news of the world's ever-altering events.

To my sister and I, both scrawny, underdeveloped and sensitive teenagers who craved all of life with its experience, its

awakening mystery and passion, the McCoy Hotel meant freedom from the confines of our female-only home, our girls-only school, and our angry, unresponding Father-God dominated religion that clouded and affected every aspect of our lives which always seemed to be on hold, waiting prayerfully for some better day, some happier time, when the three of us women would know completion, transformation, not of a self-determining kind, but one dependent upon someone else, someone who would ease us out from the unspoken prison of our lives, someone decidedly male.

All of our lives turned ever so delicately upon this unspoken tenet of unshakeable faith. To be happy you must be loved by a man. That is what my mother yearned for. That is what she taught us to desire with all our hearts.

What *I* wanted at that time was freedom from that inescapable world where one man, invisible, unresponsible, unpleasant and selfish, ruled our every waking thought, and determined every future action.

When my mother was released from her daily chores or her weekly responsibilities and discovered herself at the McCoy Hotel, her bowed back at once straightened up. She became another woman, lively, even more beautiful than she was, her long, dark-brown hair in a bun, her intense face, with its burning, deep-set brown eyes that of another woman, someone I barely knew. This new woman was open to possibility, joyful with hope.

At these times my mother was not the driven, burden-tormented, long-suffering warden of our misery, a divorced mother of two growing, demanding young women who struggled every inch of the way for individual freedom. She was someone else, almost a stranger.

My mother, having stood so much for so long, now bore the physical and emotional scars of all those years of suffering: a hunched back, bad legs with inflamed, pulsating varicose veins, an inability to sleep throughout the night, an over-reactive fear of men, all men, who could only hurt and deceive, as well as a sense of overriding anxiety that all her worst fears would come to pass. She worried if my sister and I were too close to the edge of a stairway, if we were too hot, too cold, if we were in the bathroom too long, or not long enough, if our hair was up or down, and if we did go someplace, who we were with, for how long, and why.

Our weekends at the McCoy Hotel, in downtown El Paso, were freedom to the three of us from our life in the small southern New Mexico town of Las Cruces, city of Christian martyrs, ever-present crosses.

The McCoy Hotel was just off the plaza and Mesa Street. A structure of only six stories, it seemed much taller in those days. It was situated south, facing away from the plaza toward México and the many liquor stores and *Tiendas de Rebajas*, discount used clothing stores that lined the street that became the Old Bridge we used to cross into Juárez at ten cents a car.

The hotel, while old, was quite respectable. The rooms were plain, but unusually clean for all the wildness of the border life outside its walls.

Our room had double beds that faced a moderate-sized mirror on the opposite wall, underneath which was a small basin with an overhead ledge that held two glasses turned upside down. They were wrapped in transparent, shiny, semi-waxy paper and stood next to a small pitcher of lukewarm water. That good "Texas water" my mother always bragged about.

To one side of the mirror was the bathroom door, connecting our room to that of my Tía Chita, my mother's younger sister. She lived in Redford, Texas, a town of around fifty people, where she owned, along with her seldom seen, less often heard husband, a small, but prosperous grocery store.

When we stayed at the McCoy Hotel, we invariably stayed with my aunt, who'd come into town only the night before to see her doctor, or to check up on some insurance policy or other business matter.

The two sisters were always so happy to see each other, sharing among themselves memories and stories of their days on the farm in West Texas, in a town called El Polvo, the Dust.

To my Tía Chita, El Paso was like New York City. For us, it was a new and novel, ever-expanding civilization that existed before our time and would be there long after we were gone.

In the McCoy Hotel, rooms were shared by two sets of sisters, one young, the other much older, both still working on their relationships to each other, always at odds. In the shaded darkness of those rooms, both groups of sisters sought respite from the intense summer heat, the inescapable sun, tormentingly male.

The McCoy Hotel was a meeting ground between family, a place we all came to further knowledge of our separate lives. Here we found out how deeply and irrevocably we had changed because of those secret sins we now confessed to each other. No matter how much we fought, quietly and then with anger, or how much we cried, hard to ourselves and then softly to our other sister half, the McCoy was always for us a place we loved, a place of love, despite our waning youth.

Our room and my aunt's was connected by a white and black checkered tile bathroom. It contained an old fashioned tub with heavy knobby gold splayed feet that lifted the tub high off the floor.

During the daytime, both doors leading to the bathroom remained open, allowing free access to either side of our mutual suite. At night, either side of women closed the door that led to the bathroom. When the bathroom was in use, whichever side which happened to be inside locked the door as well and ran the faucet to muffle any sounds.

I rarely went into my Tía Chita's room. It seemed very far away, despite its close proximity to us, our side, centered by those two familiar double beds, sheets crisp with starch, the blankets thin but soft.

In all the years we'd stayed at the McCoy, it never changed.

The lobby was always the same, with its red high-backed metal chairs, the paneled reception desk near the elevator, small end tables scattered here and there, with months-old magazines. The ancient, still functional elevator, with a creaky metal door you had to swing sideways, to the left, to open, locked into place once it was closed.

EEEEEEKKKKKKKKKRRRRRRRR! The metal door slid shut, the tired machine slowly revved up and creakily it ascended, coming to a not uncommon jumpy false stop as the elevator sought the right stoppage point, finally resting midway between floors. Through the firm doors with their ornate black grates could be seen a hallway, indistinguishable from the other five, with dark carpet, chairs and ceiling fan.

All those weekend visits to the McCoy Hotel melded into two strong memories. One of them was the magical time of my eagerly sought, never truly won, adolescence. I was a child then, still under the rule of my mother, who dictated my life. The other memory is as strong, and defined a period of setting forward into young adulthood, with its time of rebellion. Each of these phases marked a chapter in my life as discovered at the McCoy Hotel.

As a young teenager, I was very agitated by most everything. I felt trapped in a world I could never escape, confined to mediocrity, a pale, thin, over-protected girl to whom imagination was both fearful and a blessing. When we were at the McCoy, I became, like my mother, a new person, startled, and then emboldened by my budding maturity, and then challenged by possibility.

One afternoon, in summer, when I was thirteen, just learning to assert my growing adulthood, I left our room and wandered down the long, grey hallway. I peered down the mysterious stairs, then ran quickly, breathlessly, back to get my sister, who sat in bed, reading. My mother was in Tía Chita's room. She lay across her sister's bed, stripped down to her brassiere, wet towels holding her uncomfortably large breasts in place.

There was no air-conditioning, and all the windows were open. The ceiling fan swathed a circular path near the top of the high room, displacing and then correcting the hot air. Tía Chita, as relaxed as she ever became, wore a dark blue cotton robe and slippers, her knee-high hose held up by her soft, pink rubber-covered *ligas*, or garters. The two women talked quietly to themselves, the way people do in extreme heat, slowly, with as little breath as possible, conserving what energy they have.

Eagerly, I begged Margo to join me in my wanderings, and just as enthusiastically she replied that she would.

I liked to sneak around. I loved to be afraid. We both did. We liked to imagine things that would never come to pass. What if the building caught on fire? Who's the man in the far end room? I think he's in love with me. What if the elevator didn't work and stopped between floors and we were trapped in there with the man from the far end room? How many floors are there? Are there really only six? What if there was a secret floor that no one except us knows about? Imagine living in a hotel!

My questions grew bolder and so did my movements. Slithering through the cool, darkened hallway to the stairway, I climbed up one flight of stairs, then another, urging my little sister forward.

Afterwards, we ventured down the elevator to the lobby, controlling the lever manually. Amazement, terror and joy ruled us as we stared at the open floor moving past us. Fighting to control the lever led to us coming to a bumping and prolonged stop. Landing between floors, Margo jumped out.

More afraid, despite my age, I followed her, a somewhat timid explorer who tiptoed through the silent, tunnel-like hallway to the guest sitting room, where a solitary old man sat staring out into space.

There were no television sets or radios in the sitting rooms, much less in any of the guest rooms; the only form of entertainment was watching other human life. Few children stayed at the hotel with their parents. I never saw anyone near my age. The clientele was older, monosyllabic, long past their fecund time. The lobby clerk and his wife were elderly as well, ever polite to us, in a dry, stiff-smiling, girdle-harnessed, yellow false teeth sort of way. We jeered and made fun of them behind their backs, because we didn't know how to react to courtesy and deference from people so much older than ourselves. So, with a cruel and rude cynicism we allowed them to wait on us, little princesses come in from the heat.

In the presence of the older clerk and his wife, I felt mature, comfortable with myself, not just another person, but one younger, stronger, more alive, not exhausted and frustrated by a life nearly over, like theirs, or my mother's or aunt's, both passed over in quiet and relentless desperation; lives lived not in the present, but in a never-arriving future, with heated nightly dreams and what-might-have-been past.

I knew I wasn't so well behaved, or so nice, but what I did know was how special I was, if only to myself. I felt my life full of meaning. Surrounded by so many people, so many stories, feelings, I couldn't exactly explain why I felt so different, in the body that I wore then, an ill-fitting outer skin that wasn't really me, not the inside of me that was hidden to everyone, even myself: the spirit of the woman I longed to become.

I got off in the lobby. Margo followed. Sitting on a stiff chair, I looked out into the street, half-shaded by a set of merciful blinds, the hot sun boring small holes into my consciousness. Unable to effect longed for freedom, I returned to our room, to rest from all that longing. It tired me like nothing else ever did. Unable to explain my bad mood to Margo, I said nothing as my mother came out of the bathroom, trying on a new dress.

Pulling it over her head, the bodice stuck halfway and she called frantically to me to help her. She was trapped. Her large, humid breasts were caught in a vise of cloth. Flattened and punched down, at that moment they seemed more of a bother than something to be proud of. I was glad to be myself then, flat-chested, without that burden of softened flesh to drag around, continually subdue.

Extricating Mother from that already zippered dress took some time and was embarrassing to all three of us. Breathy, with tiny beads of sweat near her hairline, Mother was finally freed with one last tug.

My mother's large impressive body was something she could never escape, try as she might, day or night.

Nights she slept in the nude, and it was not uncommon to walk by her room to find her, head facing the window, swaddled like the statue of a carved Greek torso in her thin sheet, her wet towel draped over her prominent chest that heaved and sighed.

Did everyone's mother sleep in the nude? I didn't think so.

In that second phase of the McCoy Hotel when I was older and had begun to define myself, we stayed at the hotel for the last time.

My mother, ever-devoted chaperone, now served as a group mother to eight thespians who earlier had participated in a speech tournament in El Paso. She assigned rooms. My friend Ellen and I drew a room connected to my mother's, much to our dismay. Ellen and I slept in one adjoining room, my mother and sister in the other. The six girls were spread out between two nearby rooms, all interconnecting, with promises to behave.

I wondered: would Mother sleep in the nude this night? I hoped not.

I whispered to Ellen in the darkness.

My mother sleeps in the nude.

She does?

Yes. She sleeps with her head at the foot of her bed, her legs facing the headboard, her head near the window, so she can feel the breeze, a fan on the chest of drawers aimed at her head, her long dark hair fanned out on a small, soft pillow like a baby's under her head. Like that, nude. And when she's alone, she locks all the doors and does her housework in the nude.

No!

Yes she does. She's told me.

No!!

She says it feels good that way.

Reaaalllly?

In the summer she'll open all the windows and sleep nude with her door open all the way, the fan going all night long, forget the cost!

Really?

She gets up early before anyone gets up and goes to sleep long after anyone.

She sleeps naked?

Does your mother?

No . . . I don't . . . I don't . . . know . . .

Suddenly from the other room came a voice in the darkness. Mother had heard us!

Yes, Ellen, I sleep nude. Want to come see?

Nothing Mother said ever surprised me. I was used to her loud half-whispers, her scathing, but honest asides, her candid and profound announcements: See that woman, she needs a good bra! Look at that girl in the bathing suit, you can see her sex outlined like a man's. *Ese hombre*, that man, he smells! Puuuuuccccccchhhheeee! Excuse me, but your child is very fat, don't you think you should do something to help him?

Can't you Can't they do something about their skin, their hair, their clothes, their bra, their skirts, their pants

Hey, you there!

No one could ruffle her, no hostile salesman or rude saleslady. Mother would turn to them placidly, and with great sweetness say: You don't feel well, do you?

Nothing ever surprised me about my mother, the woman

who lay in the darkness of the McCoy Hotel, a wet wash rag on her head, a damp towel on her breasts.

She was two people to me: the potentially dangerous woman who slept in the nude, who loved to shop, try on clothes, and hit a good sale. She was also the woman who didn't feel guilty about tipping, the woman who loved going to the movies and still yearned for romance. The other woman was the woman who was my mother, preoccupied with the person she thought I should be.

The first woman I knew was bitter, hard with arthritis, never really defeated, but in constant pain of one sort or another. This woman bravely moved through her every day with actions calibrated to insure our good, pronouncing by her strict, fearful ways a burden of relationship. Her Hope or Heaven, her Garden of Eden was centered by that inescapable tree of life and love, surrounded as it was by slithering, tempting, always male serpents.

But this tormented woman, and this other life was always forgotten as we approached the McCoy Hotel.

To the immediate right of the hotel was the Plaza Theatre, constructed in the luxurious style of those days gone by. The lobby was just as elegant as the exterior. When we entered the theatre all cares left us; we forgot the harsh brightness of late afternoon El Paso.

Inside the Plaza Theatre we were transported to a world of make-believe. The theatre had a large screen that was flanked on either side by a painted facade that was lit by painted turning silver lights that blinked on and off. On either side of the screen was a mural. The one on the left depicted a beautiful Spanish señorita standing on a balcony, a rose in her hair. The opposite mural showed her suitor, a handsome, dark-haired man playing a guitar. There was an aura of yearning, unconsummated passion about the scene, as they stood separated by the huge white picture screen. There was a great and touching sadness as the viewer realized that throughout eternity the lovers would never get any closer to each other, for all the imminent drama and romance.

We usually sat in the balcony on plush red, very comfortable seats. It was an intimate and special place, as opposed to the larger lower main floor. In the cavernous darkness, I sat next to my mother, who placed herself in between Margo and me, "so you won't fight," to watch double features, and one day, four movies in a row! The movies alternated between the family type, like *The Swiss Family Robinson*, the nature or animal variety, *Ole Yeller*, the religious, *The Robe*, or there were comedies or romances like *Three Coins in the Fountain*, with an occasional hair-raising drama like *Imitation of Life* thrown in.

Mother loved the movies and so did we. Her interests extended to buying all the *Silver Screen* and *Photoplay* magazines she could afford, poring over them and passing them on to Margo and me. In our room at the McCoy Hotel we read them voraciously, never wanting anything more than to be a part of that world of glamour, intrigue, and veiled intimation.

One block away was El Colón, the Spanish speaking movie theatre, where we went to see comedies with Cantinflas or dramas with Dolores Del Río, or Pedro Infante, who was the famous Mexican singer turned movie idol. My mother loved him, and I also came to revere him. Pedro was very handsome with his thin mustache and his serious eyes. He sang to his women beautiful, wrenching songs of undying love, and they were grateful, succumbing always to his emotional, heart-filled fervor that captivated and then overcame them, but never against their wills. While I sometimes missed much of what he was saying, too embarrassed to listen closely, I secretly longed to hear those same desperate relentless words.

What El Colón gave us was passion, another form of possibility and way of living. Crying with Dolores, or Pedro, laughing with Cantinflas, I embraced my mother and her dreams, as well as those of all my people, the Mexicans and Mexican-Americans of La Frontera, the Border world that was my own. When we sat in the darkness, all our faces were familiar, laughing, crying in the same way, and the same language. We were brothers and sisters united in our world away from the Plaza Theatre, with its stately red carpets and elegant balustrades, where red-costumed blond ticket-takers greeted you in crisp English and promised you, at least momentarily, the great American dream. Somehow in Spanish, our dreams seemed purer.

At El Colón we made our way alone, of course, no usher to guide us to the sticky, paper-littered balcony, where we carved out by our insistence a comfortable place with people like us who never had to pretend who they were or how much money they had. The emotions that we experienced at El Colón were more real than those we felt at the Plaza, the stories more familiar, the language rooted in things we had experienced as women, waiting on men, one man, never quite sure if we would ever be truly loved. For an hour and a half, we could be caressed by Pedro Infante himself, who proved to all men and women that it was good to be a man, a state of being that demanded respect, especially from women. I never questioned anything then. That was in the early days of the McCoy Hotel.

In later years, I was to remember Pedro Infante, his untimely death in an airplane with his mistress. Whenever I wanted to run away with someone, this tragedy of his stayed me. I couldn't explain to myself why Pedro's death had permanently touched me. He who struggled so long in celluloid to find true love, who seemed to have found it at last in real life, only to have it snatched away so abruptly and mercilessly by a jealous God who could not condone hard won happiness, come where it had, lead where it might. An elusive attempt at joy, what others called adultery, was now a tragic character in his own life's movie.

Leaving El Colón, I always found myself immensely hungry. I begged Mother to take us down the street to the *chicharrón* place, a take-out restaurant where hot, greasy, dripping sides of pork skin hung from racks to dry. The *chicharrónes* were real, not the type with some sort of artificial preservative staining the corners with red or orange dye. They were fat, juicy, the kind I could suck for some time with enthusiasm and then crackle with my teeth. A large greasy bag went a long way. A whole side of pork skins would be broken up, and holding a treasured dollar's worth, we'd walk back to the McCoy. We'd eat them until we could eat no more, drawing the coolest water from the tap and pouring it into our glasses when we got thirsty.

From the hotel, we'd walk down to the plaza to watch the alligators that occasionally lurched outside in the hot Texas sun and then ponderously and painfully crawled back into the tepid wetness of the murky green pond, its flagstone slabs scrapping their crusted, dried underbellies. The pond, located in the center of the plaza, was inaccessible to all except these three or four closed-eyed, nearly inert alligators that inhabited that space all seasons, a displayed curiosity.

In later years, this same dusty plaza was transformed at Christmastime by an incredible display of holiday tableaus. In one, cheerful elves cavorted merrily in artificial snow while Rudolph and his cohorts pulled a smiling pale-skinned Santa through the cool desert air.

An immense Christmas tree, usually painted silver or white, stood in the middle of the plaza, where once sullen reptiles imagined freedom. Green, yellow, blue, and red alternated blinking on the tree, casting a magical spell, as excited children hovered close to impatient parents, wanting, "just one more look," at the brightly colored gift packages and little mechanical gnomes that moved staccato-like as they played tiny accordions and small tin drums, Christmas carols wafting in the air.

This is the plaza we'd drive forty-two miles to see when we were young, a tradition that in later years had little meaning. Rituals had delighted and sustained us then, like having break-fast at the Oasis restaurant next to the McCoy Hotel, where I'd order pancakes with hash browns or corned beef hash.

Sitting in a booth facing the street, my mother would contemplate her day: I need some comfortable walking shoes, a new brassiere, and my support hose, we'll go to the White House first, and then we'll have lunch at Kress' or Newberry's.

At Kress' Five and Dime, the majority of my time was spent in front of the makeup or jewelry counters. Mother roamed the store, usually ending up in the bargain basement. She'd have already picked up her supply of hairpins, hairnets, Kapock to stuff pillows, as well as some gum, and either candy orange slices or yellow gum drops that made the inside of my mouth rough if I sucked too hard.

Returning to the McCoy Hotel with our purchases, we'd rest a short while and maybe change our clothes. Shyly, and with a muffled voice, Tía Chita would call my mother from her room, someone having accidentally closed either bathroom door, to see if we were hungry. I always was. Down the creaky elevator we'd descend, my aunt included, to eat dinner at the cafeteria around the corner.

It was at this cafeteria I was first looked at as a woman, or so I imagined. Flirting with a young man over my fried fish filet, I felt him looking at me as well. Burning with embarrassment, I turned away, attempting to ignore him, and when I looked up, he was gone.

Later on, I wondered if I'd really had this exchange or not. I was in my teens, skinny-chested, wild-eyed, with a thick mop of unruly curly hair, straddled on either side by two imposing women, my mother and her sister. Could a look have gotten through?

When we returned to the McCoy, Tía Chita returned to her room. Mother closed the door to the bathroom and emerged in a flowing night gown she'd made, one size fits all. It wasn't long before she was in bed, and the night gown was on the floor, her window open to the noise of late night El Paso: the metal rattle of trucks, the screech of passing cars on their way to Juárez, and later, the constant, soothing distant lull of that border night life, that coming and going between countries, states of mind.

But before my mother's always troubled sleep, she would ask me to pull her toes. As the older, stronger one, I was inevitably asked to do this favor for her. She was arthritic, with no circulation in her battered legs, and told me it helped her to relax, just like taking hot baths from which she said she emerged ten years younger.

Taking her fleshy, bruised feet in my hands, her long second toe draped over the rest of her large feet, her Morton's toe, that had genetically become part of me as well, I would begin from the big toe and work down, pulling and popping as I went, now and then returning to a stubborn digit. Sometimes I was cruel and held my nose as I approached her, lifting her corn-filled, calloused feet irreverently as if I were holding a leprous limb.

Tired from my day, I would later join my sister in bed. We sparred awhile, fighting for control of our sleeping space.

My nights were peaceful at the McCoy, dreamless too. The days were so full, so complete, so full of variety and stimulation, that my nights were a release from the never-ending hum of El Paso, La Frontera.

After a sigh of contentment, my aunt's snores from another part of the suite would cease. I would fall asleep, under imaginary silver stars, a Spanish señorita serenaded in the moonlight.

The next morning I would wake up Mexican, glad to be myself, and yet wanting more from myself at that time than could ever be. I was my mother's vassal, my sister's companion, my father's faraway, forgotten little girl, no man's sweetheart.

Sunday morning Mass awaited me, my retribution unholy, complaining thoughts. My mother, sister and I visited many El Paso churches, never settling on one. Each unprecedented visit to an unfamiliar church allowed me one special prayer. Mother said every time you visited a new church, you could ask God for a new wish. So, I left my hopes and dreams that way, all over town.

After church we returned to the McCoy, where we left off our prayer books and gloves, and adjourned to the Oasis restaurant for more grilled cheese and tunafish sandwiches. Afterwards, Mother drove us home to Las Cruces, our city of myriad crosses.

In phase two of the McCoy, when I was older and in high school, a car full of failed debaters crowed, exuberant, if not exultant, in our blue Ford after the speech tournament. To hell with our defeats! Led by my mother we prayed the rosary. Mysterious Glory Bes led to stately Our Fathers, and onto interminable Hail Marys.

We arrived forty-two miles later, the rosary completed, merry but with crippled limbs. Never before had we fit so many girls into one car. We had set a record.

That was my last visit to the McCoy Hotel.

It's fitting that it should have been at a time of celebration for my emerging adolescent voice, a voice that then was always prone to laryngitis. I didn't know how to speak then, what to say. I was untrained, too eager to hear myself out loud, not caring whether I modulated my voice or damaged it in my fury to be heard.

My mother's voice now comes from another room. In my dreams I see her: proud, naked, dancing. She is not in her seventies as I last knew her, but young, with the beautiful full body I knew she'd always had when she was younger. She wasn't hunchbacked, as she later was, with red, always bruised feet and legs. She wasn't that anxious woman who was always wondering if my father would ever call or write, or maybe even return home. His return to us never seemed a reality. He did in fact return, the year before my mother died, and in a strange way, I believe he hastened her death, a process that had begun twenty-eight years before when he left home.

In my dreams my mother sits in our room at the McCoy Hotel brushing her long dark hair in front of an open window. I can see her from my aunt's room and yet I cannot get near. I wonder if ever, when I least expect it, she will walk into the room, and sit next to me. I will be able to smell her skin the way it was, sweet, smelling of dried flowers, overripe fruit. That is how the dying smell. It does not terrify me. I breathe in with gratitude and exhale my passing sorrow.

Several years ago I heard the Plaza Theatre was to be destroyed. The local citizenry saved it eventually, calling it an architectural landmark.

The *chicharrón* place isn't there any more, or has moved, or become one of the many Casas de Cambio that line the street leading to the bridge that will take your dollars and convert them into pesos.

After that last stay at the McCoy Hotel, we visited El Paso shortly afterward to see a visiting President Kennedy, who was staying at the Cortez Hotel, the fancy, removed stepsister of the McCoy Hotel.

The McCoy is now a remodeled office building, a place I would be afraid to go inside. Call it a phobia. Call it fear of heights. Call it whatever you like.

If I were to go inside, I would surely meet the ghosts of that past life, perhaps the solitary old man staring into space in the guest sitting room, or the phantom clerk and his wife, both aged specters, with haunting, faraway voices. Can I help you? Do you need a key?

Yes, the key!

I would see my mother inside her room, staring out the window to the oppressive heat, her ears inclining to the shouts of Viva, que viva, and there he is, the President. The hearty waves of President Kennedy are an intimation of bygone grandeur, of a mythical life, once acted out, now barely remembered, and then always with a struggle.

But I do remember.

To go back to that time is to go into the heart of the McCoy Hotel; it is to remember those thrilling, but small adventures full of imagined danger. Today they seem as lugubrious and absurd as the overheated alligators in the plaza pond. Poor creatures so far away from home!

I grew up in a world of people who were always remembering the past. When you grow up this way, time has a different significance to you than to others.

Pedro Infante, dark rebel, but for that one tragic flaw of his, was everybody's lover. He sings to me, larger than life, on the big screen in the timeless darkness of the balcony of the El Colón Theatre: *Solamente una vez* . . .

At the Plaza Theatre the Spanish señorita demurely hides her eyes while her handsome suitor sings and strums a haunting song on his guitar: *Solamente una vez* . . .

Life is spooky, but not in the ways you'd ever expect.

Grateful acknowledgment is made to the following for permission to reprint the selections in this anthology:

"The Ruins," from *Days of Plenty, Days of Want* by Patricia Preciado Martin. Copyright © 1988 by Bilingual Press/Editorial Bilingüe, Arizona State University, Tempe, Arizona. Reprinted by permission of Bilingual Press/Editorial Bilingüe.

"The Iguana Killer," from *The Iguana Killer: Twelve Stories of the Heart* by Alberto Alvaro Ríos. Copyright © 1984 by Alberto Alvaro Ríos. Reprinted by permission of Confluence Press at Lewis-Clark State College, Lewiston, Idaho.

"Doña Toña of Nineteenth Street," by Louie The Foot González. Reprinted from *Festival de Flor y Canto: An Anthology of Chicano Literature*, edited by Alurista et al., University of Southern California, El Centro Chicano, 1976. Reprinted by permission of El Centro Chicano.

"Juana Inés," by Alicia Gaspar de Alba. Reprinted from *New Chicana/Chicano Writing*, edited by Charles Tatum, University of Arizona Press, 1992. Reprinted by permission of the author.

"Abuela," by Rosa Elena Yzquierdo. Reprinted from *Revista Chicano-Requena*, Vol. 14, Nos. 3–4. Reprinted by permission of Arte Público Press, University of Houston.

"Nubes," from *Nambé—Year One* by Orlando Romero, published by Tonatiuh-Quinto Sol International, Berkeley, California. Copyright © 1976 by Orlando Romero. Reprinted by permission of the author.

"The Horned Toad," by Gerald Haslam. Copyright © 1983 by Gerald Haslam. First appeared in *New Arts Review* (January 1983); reprinted from *California Childhood: Recollections and Stories of the Golden State*, edited by Gary Soto. Reprinted by permission of the author.

"The Moths," from *The Moths and Other Stories* by Helena Maria Viramontes. Copyright © 1985 by Helena Maria Viramontes. Reprinted by permission of Arte Público Press, University of Houston.

"The Scholarship Jacket," by Marta Salinas. Reprinted from